# Project Management
# Essentials

# Project Management Essentials

Second Edition

Kathryn N. Wells, MEd., PMP
Timothy J. Kloppenborg, PhD, PMP

 BUSINESS EXPERT PRESS

*Project Management Essentials*, *Second Edition*

Copyright © Business Expert Press, LLC, 2019.

First published in 2019 by
Business Expert Press, LLC
222 East 46th Street, New York, NY 10017
www.businessexpertpress.com

ISBN-13: 978-1-94897-639-8 (paperback)
ISBN-13: 978-1-94897-640-4 (e-book)

Business Expert Press Portfolio and Project Management Collection

Collection ISSN: 2156-8189 (print)
Collection ISSN: 2156-8200 (electronic)

Cover and interior design by S4Carlisle Publishing Services Private Ltd., Chennai, India

First edition: 2015
Second edition: 2019

10 9 8 7 6 5 4 3 2 1

Printed in the United States of America.

# Abstract

Project management is seen as a critical skill across a broad range of disciplines. Yet most people, regardless of educational background, have never received training in how to plan, manage, and execute projects. *Project Management Essentials, 2nd edition*, will be the go-to book for tried-and-true project management skills combined with the most current ideas from Agile in a concise, up-to-date, user-friendly format. It follows the project life cycle and provides several ready-to-use templates. A person can use this book to plan and manage a project from start to finish or as a reference for help with one particular component of project management. Alongside each template is a brief description of what each template is, why it is useful, and an example to illustrate it.

# Keywords

Agile, leadership, project communication, project control, project management, project risk, project schedule, project teams, project success, templates.

# Contents

# Acknowledgments

We thank several sets of people for their help and encouragement as we wrote this book.

First and foremost are our family members, who inspired us to persevere: Bet, Andy, Cadence, Ellie, Nick, Jill, and Declan.

Second are our reviewers, whose insightful suggestions helped to make the book better: Stacy Decker, and Keith Sarto.

Third are the friends who contributed examples we used in this book: Raji Sivaraman and Rafael Santa Ana.

Finally, are all the colleagues, clients, and students with whom we have learned as we worked on many interesting projects.

# CHAPTER 1

# Introduction to Project Management

Welcome to *Project Management Essentials*! Whether you have been managing projects for years, are tasked with managing your first project, or are just interested in learning more about project management, this book will be a great resource for you. We'll not only go through best practices from start to finish of a project life cycle, but we'll also provide you with templates and examples from a variety of organizations.

The purpose of this chapter is to help you:

1. Describe measures of project success on your projects and use that knowledge to guide your planning and implementation.
2. Determine the project life cycle you will use, whether predictive (traditional or Waterfall), adaptive (Agile), or hybrid, along with the stages of work and approvals needed to move from one stage to the next.
3. Define major responsibilities of the key players (project manager, sponsor, core team members, and subject matter experts [SMEs] in traditional projects and scrum master, product manager, and team members in Agile projects), at each stage of your project life cycle.

In this chapter, we will introduce project management, and then discuss what project success is and what is required to achieve it. We will also introduce the concept of a project life cycle with traditional (planning),

Agile (adaptive), and hybrid variations. The final section of this chapter deals with key roles and responsibilities needed to successfully complete projects.

## What Is Project Management?

Let's start at the very beginning: What *is* a project? A project is a onetime undertaking that will result in a new product, event, or way of doing things. It will have a defined start and finish—though a project's duration could be anywhere from a few hours to many years. And just as efficient management is needed for the day-to-day activities of running a business or a household, effective project management is needed to guide any type of change. An effective project manager must be adept at overseeing the planning and work necessary to create the unique product or service prescribed by the project. In fact, the top 2 percent of project managers spend, on the average, twice as much time in planning as the other 98 percent of project managers.[1] This includes both the tasks (science) and relationships (art) needed to understand the work and keep it moving with, through, and for people.

Here are just a few of the reasons executives we've worked with have given for why project management is so important to them:

- Project management brings objectivity to projects.
- It represents an investment in current and future projects.
- It's necessary for planning and executing communication and coordination throughout projects.
- Project management helps our understanding of the big picture.
- It provides a standardized process for resolving conflicts.
- You can't run a business without project management.
- Without it, people just *assume* things.

While the tools we will show you in this book are scalable—in other words, they can be made more or less detailed to fit the size and scope of your project—they will all be based on the international standards detailed in *A Guide to the Project Management Body of Knowledge (PMBOK)*, 6th edition.

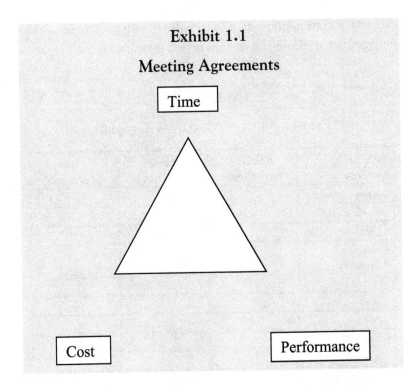

**Exhibit 1.1**

**Meeting Agreements**

## What Is Project Success?

An old rule of thumb has been that successful project completion is comprised of three factors: being on time, on budget, and achieving the specified level of technical performance. Performance includes both completing everything (called scope) and having it work correctly (called quality). These three factors (time, cost, and performance) make up a factor called meeting agreements, as shown in Exhibit 1.1. Meeting agreements is often how project managers are most closely evaluated, but it is second in importance.

The more important issue is the impact on the project customer. The very reason for performing a project is that someone or some group wants the project deliverables to use. Customer success includes customer satisfaction and successful implementation of project deliverables. Regardless of whether your customers are internal or external to your organization, their approval should be your first and foremost goal.[2,3] Sometimes additional success measures are also considered, such as other benefits to the organization and development of project participants.

## Exhibit 1.2

### Project Success Measures Template

| Success Measure | Relative Importance | How Measured | When Measured |
|---|---|---|---|
| Customer Success | | | |
| Satisfaction | | | |
| Use of deliverables | | | |
| Meeting Agreements | | | |
| Performance | | | |
| Time | | | |
| Cost | | | |
| Other | | | |
| Business | | | |
| Participants | | | |

In later chapters, we will go into greater detail about how to set and attain project success metrics. For now, begin to consider how important each success measure may be, and how and when you expect to measure it. Exhibit 1.2 is a template to help you gather your thoughts on success for your project, and Exhibit 1.3 is a partially completed success measure template for a project meant to improve the workflow in a department.

## What Is a Project Life Cycle?

Not only do all projects have starting and ending points, but they also go through similar, predictable stages that collectively make up their life cycles. A simple project life cycle includes the four stages—initiating, planning, executing, and closing—as shown in Exhibit 1.4.[4,5] The vertical dimension shows the level of effort expended (usually in number of work hours and amount of money spent). The horizontal axis shows time.

## Exhibit 1.3

## Partially Completed Project Success Measures Template

| Success Measure | Relative Importance | How Measured | When Measured |
|---|---|---|---|
| Customer Success | | | |
| Satisfaction | Very important | Survey | End of project |
| Use of deliverables | Very important | Observation | When draft method delivered; when final method delivered; and after 2 weeks of use |
| Meeting Agreements | | | |
| Performance | Important | Timing and accuracy of work process steps | When draft method delivered; when final method delivered; and after 2 weeks of use |
| Time | Somewhat important | Days ahead or behind | Weekly as project progresses |
| Cost | Less important | Dollars over or under budget | Weekly as project progresses |
| Other | | | |
| Business | | | |
| Participants | | | |

To move from one stage to another, normally an approval of some kind is needed. These typically include a charter to make the project official and grant the project manager authority; a detailed project plan to proceed; customer acceptance of the primary project deliverables; and completion of any required documentation, respectively.

Although that looks and sounds very straightforward, keep in mind that projects, by definition, are unique and thus will vary greatly from one to another. Furthermore, depending on which field you are in, the life cycle you use may be different from the generic project life cycle mentioned earlier. One of the main differences among life cycles in projects pertains to how much uncertainty there is at the start of a project. The most extreme cases are called Waterfall and Agile.

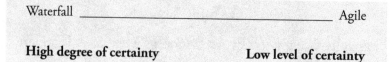

Waterfall _____ Agile

**High degree of certainty**          **Low level of certainty**

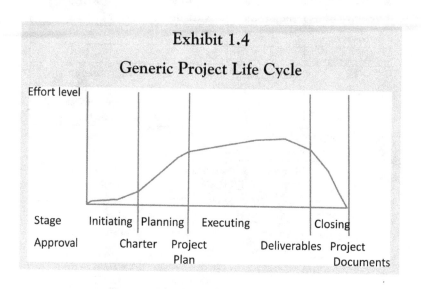

## Exhibit 1.4

## Generic Project Life Cycle

Effort level

| Stage | Initiating | Planning | Executing | Closing |
|---|---|---|---|---|
| Approval | | Charter | Project Plan | Deliverables Project Documents |

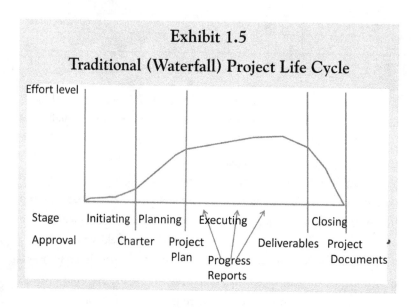

## Exhibit 1.5

## Traditional (Waterfall) Project Life Cycle

Effort level

| Stage | Initiating | Planning | Executing | Closing |
|---|---|---|---|---|
| Approval | | Charter | Project Plan   Progress Reports | Deliverables Project Documents |

Let's illustrate this point through examples. Suppose you work for a construction company, and you are tasked with the project of building a house. Although this particular house and this particular project are new to you, you've likely completed many similar projects in the past and, therefore, have a great deal of understanding of the work you need to do and the order in which you need to do it. You would be able to plan your project in its entirety before moving to the "executing" phase of the project in which you perform the work. Throughout the executing stage, you would expect to have periodic progress reports as you completed things such as design, framing, rough-ins, and so on. This is an example of Waterfall—so named because the project cascades from one stage to another in succession. A simple Waterfall life cycle is shown in Exhibit 1.5.

In terms of planning, the absolute opposite of Waterfall is the AGILE method of project management. Suppose you are a scientist working toward developing a lifesaving drug. You understand your starting point and your end goal and may have a vague idea of how to move from here to there. Yet so much of your plan will come down to the results of hypothesis testing . . . which may lead you in a new direction entirely or to tweak something you've already tried. In other words, there is a great degree of uncertainty over the life of your project. In this case, you will create a broad, overarching plan at the beginning, but you will do your more detailed planning *iteratively*, or repetitively, one bit at a time. An Agile project life cycle is shown in Exhibit 1.6. Note that it starts the same way, with a charter to authorize the project. The next main stage is to capture the customer requirements. Once this is done, the project is planned and executed in short increments called sprints. These sprints may range up to 4 weeks in duration. As one sprint is complete with accepted deliverables, the next sprint is planned and executed. A key tenet of Agile is that something of value will be delivered at the end of each sprint. Whatever project life cycle model you use, this is good advice—provide something of value early and often.

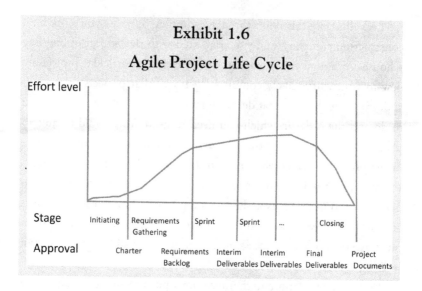

Exhibit 1.6

Agile Project Life Cycle

Another tenet of Agile is that with less detail in the up-front planning, the project team needs to be more self-organizing and self-managing. This works best with experienced and motivated workers. The project ends in a similar fashion to Waterfall in that the detailed plans are finally completed, final deliverables are accepted, and all of the administrative closing is completed.

Many organizations use some variation of a hybrid model in which the portions of the project that are easy to understand early and are unlikely to change much use a predictive approach, while the portions of the project that are unclear and/or likely to change considerably use an adaptive approach.

Predictive, adaptive, and hybrid life cycles, as well as many other industry-specific life cycles, are each equally valid, and they still have more commonalities than differences. For example, whether the planning is done entirely up front (Waterfall) or iteratively (Agile), it is essential to allow ample time for planning. In fact, the most successful project managers spend much more time on project planning than their less successful counterparts. Although it is tempting to shortchange the planning process and dive right into project execution, it will actually save you time—as well as headaches—to plan adequately from the start. Consider planning to be an investment. You can expect that the time you invest in planning will yield a return in better project execution. With that in mind, as with any investment, it is wise to evaluate carefully. Detailed planning for a large, high-risk project makes plenty of sense, but simple planning for a simple project also makes sense. We'll show you some of the most helpful project planning documents and templates in the following chapters.

## Key Roles in Project Management

Before we move on, let's take a moment to discuss the various roles in project management. We first discuss the roles in traditional project management and then identify how they differ when using Agile.

### Key Roles in Traditional Project Management

In addition to you, the *project manager*, hopefully you have executive support from your organization, in the form of a project *sponsor*. This person will oversee and champion your project throughout. She will not be the person performing the work, but she will provide guidance, encouragement, and assistance over the life of the project. Some of the ways a *sponsor* may assist a *project manager* include attending the project kickoff meeting, establishing and nurturing relationships with project *stakeholders*, signing off on major project decisions, and mentoring the *project manager*.

Keep in mind that even the best of *project managers* does not necessarily have a great deal of formal authority over the other project *team members*. There are many ways to deal with this, which we will discuss in Chapter 3. However, an adept *sponsor* will be aware of this and will facilitate interdisciplinary cooperation and preempt problems when possible or as necessary. Finally, a *sponsor* will help determine up front the project's success criteria. Even if the *sponsor* is not in the best position to make this decision herself, she needs to be in accord with the *project manager*. The *sponsor* and *project manager* will arguably be the two most essential players on the project, so it is crucial they share a common understanding of the job before them.

So what do you—or any *project manager*, for that matter—do? You will be responsible for planning and overseeing the project in its entirety. Like any good manager, you will need to prioritize, delegate, encourage, troubleshoot, and deal with change. In addition, you will use your project-specific knowledge and tools provided by this book to meet the requirements of your customer(s) and various *stakeholders*. You will lead the project team through the planning stage of the project and oversee its execution. Above all else, what you must do well is *communicate*. It is commonly accepted that a good *project manager* spends the preponderance of her work hours (maybe 80 percent to 90 percent) communicating with the project *team members, sponsor,* and other *stakeholders*. When comparing the skills most often cited in the literature as those that a *project manager* needs with the most commonly sought-after project management skills and abilities listed in job advertisements, the following six demands are at the top of both lists:

1. Communication
2. Technical skills
3. Leadership
4. Planning
5. Team building and management
6. Stakeholder management.[6]

In addition to the *project manager* and *sponsor*, a project is carried out by project *team members*. The number and function of these *team members* will vary depending on your project, but generally speaking, project *team members* fall into two categories: *core team members* and *SMEs*. *Core team members* are the workers who are assigned to the project from the earliest possible time (ideally, during the initiating stage) and stick with the project until it is either completed or terminated. *SMEs*, on the other hand, are there to help with certain parts of the project that require their input or specialized work. They can join (via "on-boarding") and leave the project team at almost any point along the project's life cycle.

Additional suggestions as to who is responsible for what at various stages throughout the project can be found in Exhibit 1.7.[7] Certainly, the *project manager's* direct supervisor may also be the project *sponsor*, but we differentiate the two roles here because that is not always the case. Also, many organizations have their own specified responsibilities for various roles that may include variations on this list.

# Exhibit 1.7

## Responsibilities of Sponsor, Project Manager, and Supervisor of Project Manager

| | Sponsor | Project Manager (PM) | Direct Supervisor of PM |
|---|---|---|---|
| Initiate | Helps identify, select, and prioritize projects; selects and mentors PM; Ensures team buy-in to charter | Writes (with team input) rough draft of charter; negotiates with sponsor | Identifies potential projects; assigns and coaches PM; helps PM develop business case for project and understand requirements |
| Plan | Meets key stakeholders; ensures PM and team perform adequate planning and effective kickoff | Creates (with team) plans for communication, scope, schedule, budget, risk, and quality; conducts project kickoff | Helps PM develop all needed plans and schedule; progressively delegates responsibility to PM |
| Execute | Proactively engages stakeholders; ensures adequate communications and emerging quality | Acquires, develops, and leads project team; manages risks and changes; monitors, controls, and reports progress | Provides continuing direction; attends progress meetings; advises PM; helps with replanning; engages stakeholders as needed |
| Close | Makes sure customers are satisfied and knowledge (technical and PM) is captured | Transitions deliverables to users; captures lessons learned; evaluates team members | Ensures lessons learned are captured and disseminated; evaluates PM; helps PM evaluate team members; signs off on project closure |
| Later . . . | Ensures promised benefits have been achieved and organization's capability has increased | Conducts follow-up assessment | Coaches PM on conducting follow-up assessment |

The structure of your organization will largely determine to whom the *project manager* will report, though most likely it will be to a functional manager or portfolio manager. In turn, your project *team members* will likely be working on more than just the project you are managing and will have their own functional managers to report to. It is important to keep this in mind because your project success largely depends on having competent, motivated workers. It would behoove you to have good working relationships with the various functional managers in your organization since you will need to negotiate with them for workers. And by respecting the fact that your workers have priorities beyond your project, you will create goodwill among your workers—workers you may very well work with again on future projects.

### How Key Roles Are Different in Agile

First, in Agile, many terms are different. For instance, instead of the names *project manager* and *sponsor*, the terms *scrum master* and *product owner* are used. Second, the terms are different to emphasize that the way they do things is often different.

The *product owner* is similar to a *sponsor* in that this person should:

- own the project vision;
- represent the business and end users;
- answer questions;
- make decisions;
- attend meetings; and
- approve work products.

The role is more involved and more continuous than that of the *sponsor*, however, in that this person should have nearly daily contact with the project team, be closely involved (or even perform personally) in defining requirements by writing the user stories that describe how the project deliverables will be used, and continuously prioritize the next most important work for the team to do.

The *scrum master* is like a *project manager* in that he:

- ensures meetings are conducted and run well;
- manages progress;
- ensures adequate and timely documentation; and
- elevates issues to be resolved.

The *scrum master* is different than a *project manager*, however, in how he:

- protects the team from distractions and overcommitting;
- ensures the team works at a sustainable pace; and—especially—
- lets the *team members* make as many decisions as possible themselves, rather than assigning them work.

Many attributes of a good *scrum master* can and should be adopted by all *project managers* such as encouraging collaboration, ensuring *team members* treat each other respectfully, and being able to usually lead in a collaborative manner, yet when in a crisis, employing a directive manner.

The Agile team is ideally comprised of full-time members who have worked closely together for a long time—maybe for multiple projects. As they develop, they should increasingly take on more responsibility so the *scrum master* is more a *team member* than a directive leader. The *team members* need to be responsible by committing to delivering certain results and then doing so. They should write their own tasks, request work, create acceptance criteria, and make decisions. They are highly empowered.

Regardless of one's role on a project, a person needs to remember that project management is a profession with expectations of ethical conduct that apply to everyone. The Project Management Institute Code of Ethics and Professional Conduct includes both mandatory and aspirational standards in the four areas of responsibility, respect, fairness, and honesty.[8] In this book, we will always conform to the mandatory standards and will often describe desired behavior that leads toward the aspirational standards.

Exhibit 1.8 is a template to help you organize your thoughts about who needs to do what and when they need to do it. You can modify this according to the project life cycle model you use, the deliverables required to move from one stage to the next, and the various participants.

## Overview of Remaining Chapters

Here is a brief overview of what to expect in the following chapters. If you are just beginning a project or are reading this to help you with projects

## Exhibit 1.8

## Project Life Cycle Roles and Responsibilities Template

| Role | Initiating | Planning | Executing | Closing | Later |
|---|---|---|---|---|---|
| Sponsor | | | | | |
| Project Manager | | | | | |
| Project Manager's Boss | | | | | |
| Core Team | | | | | |
| Subject Matter Expert | | | | | |
| Other | | | | | |

in the future, we'll follow the predictive life cycle of a project from start to finish so you can see how each of the process groups and various components are interrelated. If you need help with one particular component of project management, on the other hand, we'll provide enough instruction and examples to help you at any stage of the project life cycle.

In Chapter 2, we'll briefly touch on portfolio management, then continue on to discussing the key output of the initiating process group: the charter. Portfolio management involves strategic planning at the executive level, and although it is likely that you are not yet involved in this, we want you to understand how your project fits into the strategic vision of your organization. The second part of Chapter 2 centers on creating the charter. This is the document that sums up your project and, once agreed upon, it gives the project manager and team the authorization to pursue the project. Although the charter is generally brief (on average, only a couple of pages long), it is a crucial document that serves as the basis for all further project planning.

In Chapter 3, we'll talk about how to identify, prioritize, and engage your stakeholders. The term *stakeholder* refers to anyone with a vested interest in your project. Most projects have a wide range of stakeholders, including both those internal and external to the project. We'll also go into detail about how to manage a very special group of internal stake-holders: your project team. In addition to summarizing some of the best up-to-date management and communication strategies, we'll discuss issues unique to projects and how to best address them as the project manager. Many of the how-to's in this chapter will center around effective communication in its various forms.

Chapter 4 delves into project requirements. More specifically, *what* are people's expectations of this project, how will we meet those expectations, and how will we deal with changes that occur during the project? One of the key deliverables from this chapter is the work breakdown structure (WBS), which progressively breaks down the entirety of the project into smaller, manageable deliverables. We'll show examples of several different WBSs and guide you through the process of creating your own. We will also introduce project risk and how to plan for changes.

Chapter 5 will show you how to create a project schedule, using the WBS from Chapter 4 as a guide. We'll show you how to convert the various deliverables from the WBS into activities, which will be sequenced in a logical manner in order to create the most efficient project schedule possible. We'll then put these schedules into Gantt charts and will show you how to effectively resource your projects—addressing resource overloads where necessary.

In Chapter 6, we'll discuss the financial side to project management. We'll use best practices and examples of how to estimate cost; determine budget; and create a project baseline that integrates schedule, budget, scope, and resources. This baseline will be used to judge progress throughout the execution of your project. Upon completion of a project baseline, it will be time for you, the project manager, to schedule an official project kickoff. We'll show you how to do that, too!

Finally, Chapter 7 will coach you through directing project performance. You'll learn how to perform quality assurance and control, address project changes, and use earned value analysis (EVA) to control your schedule and budget. You'll learn effective methods of managing communications and be given corresponding templates to use or adapt. Finally, we'll walk you through the closing process group, which includes both project closing and postproject activities.

## Summary

A project is a temporary endeavor whose purpose is to create or change something. A project's life cycle will vary depending on the industry and degree of uncertainty, but generally a project moves through initiating, planning, executing, and closing phases. Each project should have a project manager to oversee the planning and work, a project sponsor to offer executive support, and a project team comprised of core team members and SMEs. To be deemed successful, a project should be completed on time, on budget, and to the agreed-upon level of quality. That said, the single most important project objective is satisfying the customer.

## Key Questions

1. How will you define and measure the project success for your projects?
2. What project life cycle model will you use, and does everyone understand the approvals needed to move from one stage to the next?
3. Who will play each key role on your projects, and do they understand their roles?

## Notes

1. Crowe (2006), p. 107.
2. Kloppenborg et al. (2014), p. 11.
3. Morris (2013), p. 16.
4. *PMBOK Guide* (2017), pp. 19–21 and 547–549.
5. Kloppenborg (2019), pp. 6–8.
6. Ahsan et al. (2013), p. 47.
7. Kloppenborg and Laning (2012), pp. 47, 80.
8. PMI (2015), pp. 53–57.

## References

*Agile Practice Guide.* 2017. Newtown Square, PA: Project Management Institute.

Ahsan, K., M. Ho, and S. Khan. 2013. "Recruiting Project Managers: A Comparative Analysis of Competencies and Recruitment Signals from Job Advertisements." *Project Management Journal* 44, no. 5, pp. 36–54.

Crowe, A. 2006. *Alpha Project Managers: What the Top 2% Know that Everyone Else Does Not.* Kenneshaw, GA: Velociteach.

Kloppenborg, T.J. 2019. *Contemporary Project Management,* 4th ed. Mason, OH: Cengage Learning.

Kloppenborg, T.J. and L.J. Laning. 2012. *Strategic Leadership of Portfolio and Project Management.* New York: Business Expert Press.

Kloppenborg, T.J., D. Tesch, and C. Manolis. 2014. "Project Success and Executive Sponsor Behaviors: Empirical Life Cycle Stage Investigations." *Project Management Journal* 45, no. 1, pp. 9–20.

Morris, P. 2013. "Reconstructing Project Management Reprised: A Knowledge Perspective." *Project Management Journal* 44, no. 5, pp. 6–23.

Nicolaas, D. 2018 *Scrum for Teams: A Guide by Practical Example.* New York: Business Expert Press.

*PMBOK Guide.* 2017. *A Guide to the Project Management Body of Knowledge,* 6th ed. Newtown Square, PA: Project Management Institute.

Project Management Institute. 2015. https://www.pmi.org/-/media/pmi/documents/public/pdf/certifications/project-management-professional-handbook.pdf, (accessed June 7, 2018).

Vanderjack, B. 2015. *The Agile Edge: Managing Projects Effectively Using Agile Scrum.* New York: Business Expert Press.

# CHAPTER 2

# Selecting and Initiating a Project

This chapter begins with the topic of portfolio management. That is, how does an organization decide what work to do and then oversee that work? A second topic in this chapter also pertains to the organizational level. Some companies have a project management office (PMO) that helps set standards and training needs, coordinates portfolio decisions, and performs other various functions to help project managers. The final topic in this chapter deals with how selected projects are initiated with simple documents called project charters. We will cover what charters are, why they are used, and what is included in a charter. We will walk you through the process of constructing your own charter and discuss the process of negotiating and getting a charter approved.

The purpose of this chapter is to help you:

1. Describe how individual projects are selected by an organization to create an optimal portfolio, subject to limits of resources and risk tolerance.
2. Create a draft project charter with enough information to make a sensible decision on whether to start the project.
3. Describe the process of negotiating a draft charter with your sponsor and committing to the project.

## Portfolio Management

If you are a project manager, chances are good that you did not choose your project but, rather, were assigned to it. Regardless, you should know at least a little about the project selection process in order to understand how your project and all the work it entails fit into your organization's strategic vision. Just as you may have a financial portfolio comprised of a variety of investments, organizations have work portfolios made up of multiple programs and projects. Organizations generally take on as much work as they can, subject to limits of resources available and risk tolerance.

And just as you have been counseled to diversify your financial portfolio, a wise organization selects a range of projects—ones of varying durations, degrees of risk, and potential for return-on-investments. Yet each and every one of these projects should reflect the values of the organization. In other words, it is through projects that an organization changes, and a thoughtful grouping of projects will move an organization closer toward alignment with its strategic values. Portfolio management includes selecting individual projects, and then prioritizing, resourcing, and governing them.

In addition to your organization's values, something else to consider when choosing projects is any gap in current abilities or products. One company we have worked with begins each year by identifying such gaps or opportunities to be exploited. They present these ideas, which they call a "roadmap," to the rest of the organization. In turn, workers propose projects designed to fill the identified gaps. In this way, the company ensures that its portfolio of projects corresponds to its business needs.

Sometimes there are external forces, such as federal or state government mandates, that will drive certain projects. For example, school districts have to upgrade their safety standards on playground equipment due to new laws around child safety. Many recreational departments and school districts were not planning to upgrade their equipment until external forces dictated they do so. These mandates are "must do" projects that become the highest priority so they can be completed by the required deadline.

## How to Propose a Project

When deciding among several competing projects, a decision maker might ask: *Where's the greatest opportunity? Which business needs are the most critical?* They will also be thinking about such things as windows of opportunity and opportunity costs, remembering that there is also a cost involved in *not* doing certain projects. If there is no clear advantage to choosing one project over another based solely on business needs, an executive may decide based on where there's the most interest and passion in her workforce, since inspired workers will likely produce a better outcome than unmotivated workers. Prioritizing decisions are not just made once; instead, they must be reevaluated as new projects are proposed and selected, older projects are completed or terminated, new market conditions arise, and a finite number of resources become stretched beyond capacity.

When proposing a project, it is helpful to remember that projects are investments of at least time, and often of money also. As such, it is reasonable to ask what benefits each potential project will bring. The best project proposal aligns with at least one organizational goal[1] and has clearly stated target benefits that appear attainable in respect to the organization's capacity and time proposed; often a leadership team of a company or division will have dozens of potential projects to consider. As such, a detailed proposal for each will likely be too much detail for them to consider, just as the project title alone may be too little. An intermediate strategy may be to have a title with a single sentence about what the project will include and a single sentence about why the project is important. Some people call this the elevator pitch—what you might quickly tell someone on a one-floor elevator trip. An example of an elevator pitch is in Exhibit 2.1.

## Exhibit 2.1
## Elevator Pitch Example

What

This project will deliver an outline of a feasibility study for the acquisition, renovation, and development of the XYZ building but will not conduct a full feasibility analysis, make the decision to purchase, or be involved with any future renovations of the building.

Why

The highly profitable ABC program is expanding and additional space is needed to support future growth and there is concern that the current owner may sell the building and force ABC out of its location.

### *How to Select, Prioritize, and Resource Projects*

One way an executive leadership team may choose among potential projects is to use a project selection matrix, then explicitly state which projects have the higher priority and ensure there are enough resources in terms of people and money with a resource matrix before authorizing a project to begin. These matrices and a description of how to use them are found in Appendix 2.

## Project Management Office

Many larger organizations have a PMO that serves as the centralized repository and decision-making body for all the organization's projects. This is useful for several reasons. First, a PMO can save project teams the trouble of "reinventing the wheel" with every project by providing useful templates and lessons learned from previous projects. In addition, the PMO has the bird's-eye view of all projects within the organization's portfolio and, therefore, can help navigate the effects of the various projects on one another. To give an example, suppose Project F is running several weeks behind schedule. The PMO (or perhaps an individual *portfolio manager* in a smaller organization) may notice that the same resources that are assigned to Project F are also assigned to Project B and can coordinate with project managers to address or mitigate the situation so that Project B is not also delayed unnecessarily. If a selection matrix was used to choose the projects, a PMO can use the scores as a reference tool at times when constraints make it necessary to put one project's needs before another's. Unless there is a compelling reason to do otherwise, the PMO will give preference to the project with the higher "score," since it would seemingly be of a higher priority to the organization.

In a similar way, PMOs can make decisions proactively to capitalize on business opportunities. Suppose a project comes along that is of far greater value to the organization than any other projects currently underway. A PMO can evaluate and reassign money, people, and other resources to the high-value project, which may delay or change other ongoing projects. While this can and should be done in some cases, a PMO should not make such a decision lightly or unilaterally. As with so many other project management situations, effectively communicating with stakeholders (especially the projects' sponsors and project managers) is paramount. If a worker's project is delayed or suspended through no fault of their own, he or she deserves an explanation why. Hopefully an up-front account of the critical business need will go a long way toward assuaging any negative feelings brought about by an abrupt change.

## Initiating Projects with a Charter

We referred last chapter to the project life cycle. Regardless of which life cycle your organization uses, the first stage is to *initiate* the project. Once your project has been selected and the key players have been assigned—at least the project manager and sponsor, and preferably the project team as well—there are two main things you must do before moving on to the more detailed planning: identify stakeholders and create the project charter.

### Why Use Charters?

A project charter serves a few key purposes. First, it helps give everyone involved a common understanding of what the project entails and why it is being done. Second, it includes preliminary estimates of budget, risks, milestone schedule, and approval requirements. Collectively, this information can help a busy executive or other decision makers decide whether or not it makes sense to "green light" the project prior to a substantial investment of time and/or resources. Finally, the signing of the project charter authorizes the project manager and her team to proceed with the project. Though a charter is nonbinding, it represents a good-faith intention of all involved to further plan and successfully complete the project.

To be blunt, without a clear understanding of *what* the project is and *why* it is important, your team and your project will be in trouble. It is better to hash out an agreement now and have everyone commit to it by signing the charter than it is to get further along the project life cycle without clear focus or vision. As one of our client companies frames it, "If we are successful, what will that look like?" If it seems absolutely impossible for your team to reach an agreement on the scope overview and business case of your project, you may need to abort or amend the project. Doing so now, in the initiation phase, will prevent you from assigning resources to an ultimately doomed project. This represents one further reason to create charters—to help cut losses early by weeding out projects that are unnecessary or out of alignment with the organization's strategic goals.

## What Is Included in a Charter?

Typical components of a project charter often include the three *W*s, *R*s, and *C*s as shown in Exhibit 2.2.[2]

### Exhibit 2.2
### The Three Ws, Rs, and Cs of Project Charters

| 3 Ws | 3 Rs | 3 Cs |
|---|---|---|
| **What** (scope overview) | **Risks** | **Communication needs** (stakeholder list) |
| **Why** (business case) | **Resources** | **Collection of knowledge** (lessons learned) |
| **When** (milestone schedule with acceptance criteria) | **Routines** (team operating principles) | **Commitment** (signatures) |

The *what* section describes what the project will create and often also specifies what the project will *not* create. This helps everyone understand how big the project is. The *why* section describes the reason for undertaking the project. These first two sections are the "elevator pitch" described earlier. Now, let's discuss the *when* milestone schedule with acceptance criteria. When we refer to milestones, we mean a handful (generally no fewer than three and no more than eight) of intermediate points over the life cycle of your project, at which it is possible to measure progress by having someone assess the emerging project quality. The most useful milestones involve a deliverable or handoff from one worker to another. Identifying these milestones in advance—along with the quality and completeness you hope to see at each milestone and who will determine it—will keep your project headed in the right direction from the onset. On Agile projects, the planning and executing will occur in increments called sprints. Each sprint, usually lasting 2 to 4 weeks, will end with one or more deliverables with acceptance criteria. Since the detailed understanding of the work evolves, the exact deliverables and acceptance criteria are only determined one sprint at a time and are not known when the charter is developed.

*Risks* are either threats or opportunities. Yes, according to *A Guide to the Project Management Body of Knowledge (PMBOK Guide)*, risks can be positive! Risks are events that may or may not happen, and *if* they happen, they are likely to impact your project.[3] *PMBOK Guide* often groups constraints and assumptions together. Basically, what are your limiting factors and what do you *believe* to be true, though you do not have proof?[4] A few examples of constraints could be a 40-hour workweek, a limited number of workers, or a season in which the work must be performed. An example of an assumption might be that construction workers will not work on rainy days.

*Resources* are the people, money, and other resources that must be used to complete the project. Remember projects are investments. The resources describe what you invest in the project while the *what* and *why* sections describe the benefits you hope to receive.

*Routines* are how the team plans to work effectively together. This is especially emphasized on Agile projects as it is critical for team members to work as a mostly self-directed team.

*Communication needs* list the stakeholders and what each wants and hopes to gain from the project. This is critical since many projects run into trouble due to poor communications.

*Collection of knowledge* consists of the project team looking back at previous projects to determine ways they can be more effective on this project by applying lessons they have learned.

The *Commitment* box is where the sponsor, project manager, and core team sign to publicly commit to the project.

Remember, you will expand on each of these descriptions soon, during the planning process. Right now, keep everything simple and concise. Also, keep in mind what we said about project documentation being *scalable*: a large project may require each of these sections and more, while a small project may require just a scope statement and business case (the *what* and the *why*). Either way, you will reserve the more detailed planning for if and when the project charter is signed. In fact, that signing of the charter is what will take you from the initiating phase of the project to the planning phase.

### *How to Construct a Charter?*

Assuming you can find agreement on the *what* and *why* of your project, you should conduct a brainstorming session with your entire team and, if needed, subject matter experts. Creating the charter is one time that subject matter experts are often consulted because they can help provide knowledgeable opinions and estimates on the various components of the charter. In addition, if you can, get your customer or end user involved as early as possible in the project. Remember, satisfying the customer is your paramount goal, so getting their input about the parameters of the project will pave the way toward meeting this objective.

We find an effective way to start is to have the person who knows the most about the project to just start telling everything he or she can about their vision of the project including what might be included and why. A second person can capture those ideas on a flip chart, marker board, or computer, while a third person asks clarifying questions to help everyone understand. This does not need to be organized – it can be stream of consciousness.

### *What* and *Why*

Channel the "why" ideas your group identified into a two to four sentences business case that explains the purpose of the project. The best business case statements include how the project is aligned with an organizational goal; what kind of return-on-investment to expect; an emotional appeal; and/or an ethical imperative as to why the project must be done.

Next, use your common understanding of the "what" to write a scope overview of the project. This statement should also be about two to four sentences. A great scope overview describes clear boundaries of what will be included in the project and what will not. Quantifying the project by size or number—even if the size is a guess at this point—also helps decision makers understand how big the potential project will be.

### When

The next section is the "when"—the milestone schedule with acceptance criteria. This section will have four columns with headings of milestone, completion date, judge, and acceptance criteria. Your first step as shown in Exhibit 2.3 is to state the current situation in three or four words at the first line in the first column. This can be distilled from the "why" statement. For the second step, skip to the end and in three or four words describe the successfully completed project in the last line in the first column. (If the project is part of a larger ultimate goal, list the ultimate goal below the project ending row.) For the third step, remain in the bottom row and proceed to the right to the last two columns. Here you will state who will judge the project and what criteria they will use.

Only once you have filled out the final milestone with corresponding success criteria and judge should you go back and identify milestones (step 4). Do this by identifying three or four places between the start and finish where progress can be judged in terms of both schedule and quality. List these as milestones in rows of the first column. For step 5, next to each milestone, in the third and fourth columns, list who will judge each and what criteria they will use. Finally for step 6, estimate the dates when you hope to reach each milestone.

## Risk

Next you will identify, assess, and plan for risks. To identify risks, have each person brainstorm as many risks (though risks can be positive or

## Exhibit 2.3

### Milestone Schedule with Acceptance Criteria Template with Steps

| Milestone | Completion Date | Judge | Acceptance Criteria |
|---|---|---|---|
| Current Situation | | | |
| | | | |
| | | | |
| | | | |
| | | | |
| Future State | | | |
| ↓ ↓ Ultimate Goal | | | |

negative, generally this risk identification will focus on potential threats, or negative risks) as they can and write each on its own Post-it note. Once your team has identified as many risks as possible, create a large chart (as shown in Exhibit 2.4) with the y-axis representing the probability from low to high the a risk will occur and the x-axis representing the impact the risk event will have if it occurs, again from low to high. Understanding that the total risk for any single event is the probability it will occur times the impact if it does, the team will use a concave line to separate the major risks from the minor ones. With you or another team member serving as facilitator, the team should jointly agree where each risk falls on the chart, in terms of probability and impact. Finally, your team will develop one or more response plans for each of the identified major risks and assign one person on your team or even your sponsor to watch for the risk and implement the response plan if needed. The three major risks appear in the response plan portion of the charter in Exhibit 2.5.

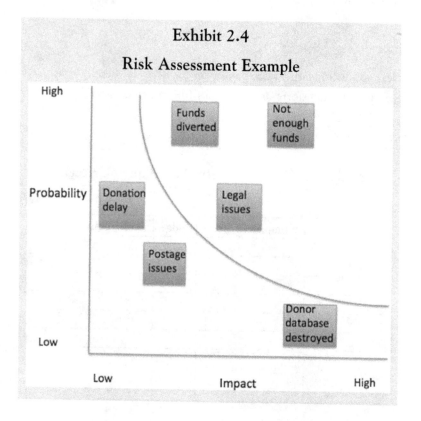

## Exhibit 2.4

## Risk Assessment Example

## Resources

After risks, describe the resources you will need to perform the project. This can include people, money, and other resources such as space or equipment.

## Routines

Next consider the routines the project team will need to follow to be successful. These generally include ideas on how to smoothly make decisions, run meetings, treat each other with respect, and perform the project work on a sustainable basis. If your team has worked together before or if your organization has clearly spelled out and accepted team methods, refer to those and use them. If not, decide how you will proceed. In project management, these are referred to as your team's "ground rules."

## Communication Needs

For the next section of your project charter, brainstorm a list of individuals and groups who may be interested in your project. These are your stakeholders and will determine your project communication needs. As a team, you should identify what each stakeholder cares about and determine which stakeholders are most important to your project.

## Collection of Knowledge

Your team should look at previous projects to determine what worked well that you can copy or modify, and what worked poorly that you will avoid. These are the *lessons learned*, and by using them consistently, your projects will run better and better.

## Commitment

Finally, you will want to include a spot for the sponsor, project manager, and core team members to sign the charter.

An example charter is shown in Exhibit 2.5.

# Exhibit 2.5

## Project Charter Example

**Project:** Create Fundraising Plan for McKinley High School Performing Arts Building

**What (Scope Overview):** This project will create a plan to attract capital and evaluate possible revenue streams including fundraising activities and a communications plan to finance a new-performing arts center. The center, using the concept design approved by the school board, will be state of the art and is expected to cost about $6 million. This project will end with the fundraising plan. If approved, future projects would raise the funds and build the building.

**Why (Business Case):** Art is an important educational component promoting self-expression, independence, and cooperation. McKinley has a state-recognized theater program, but inadequate facilities that are shared with athletics. A new-performing arts center will provide dedicated stage, classroom, and display space to enable more productions and further build the McKinley brand.

## When (Milestone Schedule with Acceptance Criteria)

| Milestone | Completion Date | Judge | Acceptance Criteria |
|---|---|---|---|
| **Current State:** Design approved, no funds raised | | | |
| Funding channels identified | 2/28 | Sponsor | Comprehensive, worst and best identified |
| Revenue-generating plan drafted | 3/15 | Sponsor | Realistic, covers full $6 million |
| Fundraising activities determined | 3/31 | Professional Fundraiser | Each activity detailed |
| Communications plan drafted | 4/30 | Principal | Can be used to reach funders |
| **Future State:** Final funding plan and revenue stream plan approved | 5/31 | School Board | |
| **Ultimate Goal:** Using new center | | | |

# Risks

| Risks | Risk Owner | Contingency Plans |
|---|---|---|
| Not enough funds generated | Sponsor | Create emotional appeals Build smaller facility |
| Funding not secured or diverted | Sponsor | Follow-up within 48 hours of commitment |
| Legal issues | School board | Document intended use when receiving funds |

# Resources

| Money | People | Other |
|---|---|---|
| $6 million for building | School Committee | Branding for fundraising |
| $10,000 for fundraising | Construction Firm | Construction Equipment |
| | Alumni | Building Site |

# Routines (Team Operating Principles)

- Every opinion counts.
- Commit to timeline.
- Come to meetings prepared.
- Be transparent with frequent updates and info sharing.
- Deliver our best.

# Communication Needs (Stakeholders)

| Stakeholders | Interest in Project |
|---|---|
| Primary: Theater Department, Band and Choir School committee with principal, Boosters with sponsor | Place for rehearsal and shows Enough funds, allow programs to flourish |
| Others: Athletic Department Community Theater | Worry about their own funding and land use Could take away shows, could serve as backup |

# Collection of Knowledge (Lessons Learned)

- Up-front communication on alignment and expectations are critical
- Involve all stakeholders early and with updates
- Ensure school board, principal, and impacted departments are fully committed

## Commitment

| Sponsor | Date | Signature |
|---|---|---|
|  |  |  |
| Project Manager | Date | Signature |
|  |  |  |
| Core Team Members | Date | Signature |
|  |  |  |
|  |  |  |
|  |  |  |

### *Approving the Draft Charter*

Once the project manager and team have constructed a draft charter, the next step is to present it to the sponsor. Often the sponsor will question some of the charter. Sometimes the team will be asked to present the charter to a group of executives, not just the sponsor. Regardless of whether the decision maker is a single sponsor or a group of executives, it is helpful to remember the team is selling on three levels:

- First, they are selling the project by trying to show that the results will be worth the investment.
- Second, they are selling their approach as one that has a good chance of being successful.
- Third, they are selling their own capability to be the right people to perform the project.

After a discussion, the sponsor, project manager, and team should reach an agreement on the charter and then sign it. Once they sign, they should feel committed to the concept of the project (because the detailed planning has not yet started, they cannot commit to the detail). Everyone should then do their best to plan and execute the project. A charter template is shown in Exhibit 2.6.

# Exhibit 2.6

## Charter Template

Project Charter

**Project Title** _____ **Date** _____

**What** (Scope Overview) (2 to 4 sentences about what is included and what is not)

**Why** (Business Case) (2 to 4 sentences with return-on-investment, alignment, emotional appeal, ethical imperative)

**When** (Milestone Schedule and Acceptance Criteria)

| Milestone | Completion Date | Stakeholder Judge | Acceptance Criteria |
|---|---|---|---|
| Current Situation | | | |
| | | | |
| | | | |
| | | | |
| End-of-Project Situation | | | |
| Ultimate Goal | | | |

## Risks

| Project Risks | Risk Owner | Contingency Plans |
|---|---|---|
| | | |
| | | |
| | | |
| | | |

## Resources Required

| Money | People | Other |
|---|---|---|
| | | |
| | | |
| | | |

## Routines (Team Operating Principles)

- _____
- _____
- _____

## Communication Needs (Stakeholders)

| Stakeholders | Interest in Project |
|---|---|
| Primary: | |
| Others: | |

## Collection of Knowledge (Lessons Learned)

- _____
- _____
- _____

## Commitment

| Sponsor | Date | Signature |
|---|---|---|
| | | |
| Project Manager | Date | Signature |
| | | |
| Core Team Members | Date | Signature |
| | | |
| | | |
| | | |

Some companies have a structured approach to charter approval and the kickoff of the detailed project planning and project execution. At least one successful company we know of makes a practice out of blowing up the signed charter to several times its original size and posting it on the wall of the "war room" where the project team meets and works. This makes it easy when there is a disagreement about the project to refer to the original charter for guidance—and to remind people of their commitment to the project.

# Summary

Organizations use projects to change and grow. Therefore, the projects an organization chooses to undertake should be in line with the organization's values and overall strategy. Organizations that perform many projects often have a centralized PMO to coordinate project resources and provide support for project teams. Project proposals should always begin with the business case (*why*) and scope statement (*what*). A project charter is used to create a common understanding among the project team and other stakeholders about some of the key aspects of a project (i.e., scope, risks, stakeholders, milestones). By signing the charter, a project team commits to moving forward with the planning and execution of a project and the project's sponsor provides the official authorization for the project to begin.

## Key Questions

1. How are projects proposed and selected in your organization?
2. What templates, standards, or other advice is given in your organization for creating charters?
3. How is agreement and commitment reached between sponsors, project managers, and core teams on charters in your organization?

## Notes

1. Zwikael and Chih (2014), p. 9.
2. Kloppenborg and Laning (2012), pp. 51–53.
3. *PMBOK Guide* (2017), p. 720.
4. *PMBOK Guide* (2017), pp. 699–701.

## References

Kloppenborg, T.J., and L.J. Laning. 2012. *Strategic Leadership of Portfolio and Project Management.* New York: Business Expert Press.

*PMBOK Guide.* 2017. *A Guide to the Project Management Body of Knowledge,* 6th ed. Newtown Square, PA: Project Management Institute.

Zwikael, O., and Y. Chih. 2014. "Project Benefit Management: Formation and Appraisal of Target Benefits." In *Proceedings Project Management Institute Research and Education Conference,* Phoenix, AZ.

# CHAPTER 3

# Engaging Your Team and Other Stakeholders

Projects are conducted with and for many people. This includes team members who do the work, as well as stakeholders who have an interest in the project's process and/or results. This chapter deals with understanding and working effectively with both your team and all other stakeholders.

The purpose of this chapter is to help you:

1. Work through typical issues that project teams face.
2. Effectively acquire, develop, and lead your team.
3. Identify, prioritize, communicate with, and build relationships with project stakeholders.

## Your Team

A project team is a select group of individuals with complementary skills and disciplines who work together on interdependent and interrelated tasks for a predetermined period to meet a specific purpose or goal.[1] As we mentioned in Chapter 2, ideally the entire project team will be involved early on in the life cycle of the project and can help draft the charter. Helping to shape the project by being involved in this early planning will foster a sense of ownership and commitment to the project. If, however, it is simply not possible to involve certain team members during the initiation phase of the project, you will need to find other ways to secure their commitment. These may include asking for their input in further planning and uncovering their preference of work assignments. It also includes always acting ethically as a project manager and not overworking your team members (or overpromising results, since that will inevitably strain your workforce). Finally, whether the team members were able to help craft the charter or not, they should each take the time to read and understand it, then sign their names to it as a public sign of commitment to the project.

## Typical Issues with Project Teams

One issue faced by many project teams is the fact that the project manager has limited direct control over the other team members. On many projects the team members work part-time on the project and will be evaluated by their functional supervisor. We encourage project managers to furnish well-written input for team members' evaluations—and let the team members know well in advance your intention to do so. The project manager can even say: "I know your manager is very busy and if I write the evaluation well enough, part of it is likely to be cut and pasted into your official evaluation." Project managers can also make up for their limited formal authority by using other forms of power. If they are seen as an expert, a friend, or someone who has high-level connections (such as with the sponsor), team members are more likely to willingly follow. Of course, the opportunity to work on an exciting project with an inspiring purpose and challenging work motivates many team members, as well.

Resource sharing is another typical project issue. Many participants are assigned to multiple projects in addition to their ongoing work. There is often a struggle to get the team member's undivided time and attention when needed. A related issue is multitasking; while multitasking is extremely common and sometimes necessary, it is usually not very productive. A good project manager will try hard to understand the various commitments of her team members and strive to find ways to limit the need for multitasking.

Potential misunderstandings are frequent on project teams. Some of this stems from uncertain and changing requirements. Investing time in really understanding requirements and having a firm change control process help in this regard. This process is described with an example in Chapter 7. Some misunderstandings occur because team members may be different in respect to education-level, experience, location, age, and so on. Diverse project teams generally are good since different skills and perspectives are needed, but they can lead to confusion. Conflict management may be required occasionally.

Yet another typical project team issue is location. At one end of the spectrum is co-location, which as the name implies, involving the project team sharing a work area. This is ideal from the standpoint of sharing information and for team members' general development. It may *not* be ideal in terms of team members' technical development, as the one engineer assigned to the project will spend most of her time on the project with people from other disciplines rather than with other engineers. At the other end of the spectrum are virtual teams. These can include people in multiple time zones and continents. Each of the typical project team challenges can be amplified with virtual teams since communication can be difficult. For this reason, the good project management practices described in this book are even more essential on virtual teams. Additionally, if the team is able to meet even once face-to-face, many of the potential problems can be more easily resolved since the team members feel a stronger connection to each other.

## Identify Team Member Needs and Secure Commitment

For some projects, there is really no choice as to who will be on the team because the organization is small and/or the needs are very specific. When there is a choice, however, the first thing to do is to determine the project's needs in terms of skills, representation, and size. Small project core teams have an easier time with scheduling and making decisions. They are also less expensive than large teams. If a large number of constituencies need to be represented, it may be best to have a smaller team with each team member responsible for coordinating with two or three of the stakeholder groups. As a project manager, you need to make sure the potential team member really is capable of understanding the needs of those two or three groups. Project managers need to understand enough about the technologies that will be used on the project in order to determine the necessary skills needed. In identifying people who may have those skills, talking with other managers and key experts will be helpful.

Once potential team members are identified, it makes sense to interview them. Part of the interview is to ask questions to understand the person's attitude and skills. Helpful characteristics to look for include commitment, flexibility, sense of urgency, and trust in you as a project leader. Your project team is comprised of the core team members who will be with your project from the beginning to end and the subject matter experts (SMEs) who will be brought in for specific tasks or durations. If a person has a unique skill within the organization and must be on the project team, you may ask him if he wants to be on the core team (and thus responsible for attending all meetings and doing project work between meetings). If so, he would be a core team member and would contribute to project decision making. If he is not willing or able to be a core team member, he would be a SME. As such, he would be invited into one or more planning meetings to offer input concerning his part of the project and would be invited to return to implement his part of the work. However, he would not be part of making project-wide decisions.

As part of the interview, the project manager should share her vision for the project, helping the potential team member understand how the project helps to further organizational goals. A good project manager will also be upfront about asking: *What do the team members hope to gain from the project?* By understanding what motivates each team member—money? Building skills for the résumé? Personal recognition?—an adept project manager can often create win–win scenarios in which the project workers are well-matched with the work assigned to them. This will create an engaged team and serve you well in the long run as a project manager, since workers will remember and be eager to work for you again.

### Develop Your Project Team

Tuckman's project team development model of *forming, storming, norming, performing*, and *adjourning* can be used to visualize how project team members can develop maturity, relationships, attitudes, and skills.[2] Exhibit 3.1 shows a few of the team process methods and a few of the ways in which team members develop both their attitudes and skills by working on a well-led project team.[3] Leading your team in a collaborative style will allow the members to gel as a team and to develop both skills and attitudes that will help the project succeed.

## Exhibit 3.1

## Project Team Maturity, Relationships, Attitudes and Skills Development Stages

| Stage | Forming | Storming | Norming | Performing | Adjourning |
|---|---|---|---|---|---|
| Team process methods | Signed commitment in charter | Role assignments, team ground rules | Collaboration, assessments | Lessons learned, meeting management | Celebrate, reward |
| Maturity, Relationships, and Attitudes developed | Excitement, skepticism | Questioning, then commitment | Part of team, success will happen | Close to team, improve self | Maintain relationships, seek next challenge |
| Skills developed | Create charter | Create all needed plans | Manage trade-offs | Report progress, update plans | Validate deliverables |

### Lead Your Project Team

Lead your project team by example! Both job advertisements and project management research agree that six of the most important competencies project managers need to use are communications, technical skills, leadership, planning, team building, and stakeholder management.[4] So, how does a project manager display these competencies in useful ways? By how they act, by what they say, and by the questions they ask.

Things you can do as project manager to effectively help lead a team include the following:

- Stand up for your team and their ideas.
- Serve your team rather than the other way around.
- Review plans and reflect, yet show a sense of urgency.
- Only promise what you can deliver and keep your promises.
- Find alternative ways around obstacles.
- Strive to understand the whole situation.

- Stay focused.
- Enjoy your work and let it show.
- Do good quality work.
- Volunteer to help those who are struggling.
- Keep the big picture clearly in sight.
- Plan and conduct effective meetings.
- Create psychological safety for your team members.

Ways of communicating as a project manager to effectively help lead a team include the following:

- Communicate openly and honestly.
- Investigate to find the truth, then communicate it.
- Admit and learn from your mistakes.
- Treat everyone fairly.
- Speak calmly.
- Make requests instead of demands.
- Don't complain about what cannot be changed.
- Acknowledge when something is done well.
- Handle negative situations in a positive manner.

Project managers can ask questions such as the following at selected milestones and during the closing of the project:

- Do/did you understand the mission and goals of the team?
- Do/did you understand your role?
- Is/was your tasking specific enough?
- Do/did you understand how your input contributed to the goal of the project?
- Are/were the team meetings effective and timely?
- Do/did you feel you were respected and your thoughts listened to?
- Is/was the communication open and honest?
- Do/did you feel the team environment (meetings and interactions) was too informal or formal?
- Do you have any ideas on how to improve?[5]

# Identify and Prioritize Stakeholders

## Who Are My Project's Stakeholders?

In identifying stakeholders—that is, the people who may impact or be impacted by a project—most of us are quick to identify at least a couple. It is obvious to most that the customer or end user as well as the project manager and team members are project stakeholders. However, on even a relatively small project, that may be just scratching the surface.

Why is it important to know who our stakeholders are? A project's stakeholders may vary greatly and include stakeholders internal to and external from the project, those in favor of the project and those opposed to it, those impacted by the final project outcome or product versus those affected by the process, and so on. Regardless, by learning from and effectively communicating with our various stakeholders throughout the lifecycle of the project, we greatly enhance our chances of project success.

## How Do I Prioritize My Project Stakeholders?

Keeping in mind the facts that stakeholders want different things from a project and that even the most popular projects generally face some opposition, you can see why you need to not just *identify* but also *prioritize* your stakeholders. When push comes to shove, whose support and approval is essential to the project? These are your key stakeholders, and you need to do everything you can to keep them informed and favorably disposed toward the project.

Beyond the key stakeholders, it is still helpful to put all other stakeholders (or groups of stakeholders) into a rough order of importance. Again, this order of importance exists so that in times of challenge or conflict, when all stakeholders' hopes and expectations cannot be met or are even in conflict, you will be prepared to make the tough decisions in the best interests of your project and its most important stakeholders.

Now, the term "most important" stakeholders will have different connotations for each project or team. You will need to decide—along with your sponsor—how to compare and categorize stakeholders according to the following criteria: power to affect the project's outcome and interest in the project process and/or project results. Exhibit 3.2 shows the relative power and interest of various stakeholders.

## Exhibit 3.2
## Project Stakeholder Power Interest Grid

| | | Interest | |
|---|---|---|---|
| | | Low | High |
| Power | High | High Power, Low Interest<br>– Keep Satisfied<br>• Marketing Manager | High Power, High Interest<br>– Manage Closely<br>• Operations Manager<br>• General Manager<br>• Finance Director |
| | Low | Low Interest, Low Power<br>– Apathetic<br>• Team members working on-site | Low Power, High Interest<br>– Keep Informed<br>• Team leads working on-site |

One further stakeholder consideration is this: on projects where stakeholder influence is high, merely communicating with them is not enough. The project team members need to understand the impact the project will have on the stakeholders and interact with them and make decisions accordingly. Exhibit 3.3 illustrates this.

## Exhibit 3.3
## Type of Project Considering Stakeholders[6]

| | Stakeholder Neutral | Stakeholder Sensitive | Stakeholder-led |
|---|---|---|---|
| Stakeholder power and influence | low | medium | considerable |
| Key project challenge | technical | some stakeholders need to make some changes | many stakeholders need to make big changes |
| Project team needs to: | identify and communicate with stakeholders | consider stakeholder agendas when selecting best approach | determine solution based upon what stakeholders will allow |

Finally, keep in mind that prioritizing stakeholders requires as much art as science, and a good project manager can help his team think outside the box. Instead of assuming that any stakeholders opposed to your project are entrenched in their opinions, ask yourself—or, even better, ask *them*—if there is anything you could do to either win them over to supporting your project or, at least, to lessen their opposition to it. Exhibit 3.4 is from a project management student of ours and is one of the best examples of proactive stakeholder management we have ever seen.

## Exhibit 3.4

## Building Relationships with Stakeholders

*CIDEC is a Design and Engineering Center which employs 250 Engineers, Masters, and Ph.D.'s, located in the suburbs of the city of Queretaro, Mexico. This example is provided by Rafael Santa Ana, general manager of the Queretaro Technical Center:*

We develop product and process design for automotive electrical components and its related embedded software.

Our product lines include:

- Wiring harnesses;
- Information and entertainment systems;
- Passive safety (seatbelt and airbag sensors and controls);
- Active safety (radars, cameras, self-braking systems);
- Hybrid vehicle power electronics.

Our building is located in an area zoned as "commercial, offices, or light industry use." Across the street it is zoned as "residential use only." We obtained the required government permits and started construction of our new facility, only to have the neighbors' owner association from across the street go to the City Hall to complain about our building, fearing that we would be noisy, smelly, traffic obstructing, and so on.

It dawned on us that the neighbors were stakeholders in our new building project, since our presence there would have an impact on their lives. We immediately contacted them and explained our project to them, apologizing for not having done so in advance. We showed them that we were only offices; our parking lot was big enough for all our employees; and there would be no noise from our processes to negatively impact them.

We invited them to use our cafeteria with its tables, chairs, projector, restrooms, vending machines, parking area, and so on. They accepted. We then extended our offer for them to use our cafeteria for all their meetings, which they also accepted.

During one of their meetings we asked them if there was anything we could do to be better neighbors. At night one of our lamps also illuminated the children's bedroom of a couple of houses, so that the kids did not want to go to sleep. We turned off or reoriented the lamps. Another request was to reduce the noise level of the automatic water pump, which sometimes turned on in the middle of the night. We placed a sound proof cover on top of it.

When our employees hired a yoga instructor and started to practice, we asked the neighbors if they were interested and some of them joined the classes. We also have Ping Pong, table soccer, and chess competitions, which some of the neighbors have joined. Employees of ours have a cross-country hiking club and a cycling club which some neighbors have joined.

Since we compost all the leftovers from our cafeteria, we offered compost bags for the neighbors' gardens and showed them how the process works. Now they have their community compost.

Some of our employees took first aid, first responder, and firefighting training, and are prepared to help in medical emergencies (heart attacks, fractures, burns, heat stroke, etc.) until professional help arrives in an ambulance. We shared with the neighbors their contact numbers. We have 24/7 security personnel at our reception area. We asked our security personnel to look at the neighbors' homes during their rounds and to contact them and the police in case of suspicious activity. So far we have had no need to do that.

Some of our neighbors' sons or daughters are studying or planning to study engineering. We invited them to visit us to see what a day at work for an engineer looks like. They came with a school bus full of students! They are also among the interns and full-time recruits we've had since opening this location.

The home-owners' association continues to meet monthly at our facilities, and every time we ask them if there is anything else we can do to enhance our mutual relation. Their feedback is very positive and they tell us that we are positively impacting their lives with our operation.

### *How Do I Communicate with My Project Stakeholders?*

Now is as good a time as any to talk about project communications. It has been estimated that a good project manager spends up to 90 percent of her time communicating.[7] 90 percent! This includes reading, writing, and **listening**. That said, quantity is no replacement for quality when it comes to communications. In fact, communication that serves no useful function for all participants—a pointless meeting; weekly status reports that no one ever reads; e-mails that *cc* countless people unnecessarily—not only waste time that could be better spent, it also frustrates workers and other stakeholders. The reason we communicate on projects is "communication leads to cooperation, which leads to coordination, which leads to project harmony, which leads to project success."[8]

Too many organizations and individuals act as though the information age never dawned and that people need *as much* data and information as possible. While we are not suggesting withholding any needed or relevant information, too often it is the deluge—not the lack—of data which overwhelms and slows people down. What people really need is an overarching understanding of the entire project and the information pertinent to their work, in a format that is easy to understand. That is to say, do not overwhelm your workers with mountains of raw data but, rather, convey to them useful information in a timely manner—and make sure your communication is a two-way street.

One frequent complaint we hear is in regard to some organizations' tendencies to create "silos" in which there are only a limited number of people with whom any worker is allowed to communicate (generally this includes direct report but not cross-disciplinary relationships). We encourage you and your project team—and even your organization as a whole—to foster a culture that values direct communication whenever possible. This will help ensure that your messages are communicated as intended (think of the children's game *Telephone* as the epitome of what you *do not* want to happen!), without confusing or overwhelming people who don't need to be involved. Workers and stakeholders both need only as much timely information as they can reasonably process while still being responsible for many other competing demands on their time and energy. Keep this in mind as you are managing your team and communicating with them and other stakeholders.

Agile promotes effective communication culture by stressing frequent in-person meetings, mitigating distraction, using feedback to ensure the message is clearly understood, having key business stakeholders on the project team, and creating the *Agile trust factor* with foreflow of ideas without value judgments.[9]

Best practices suggest that you plan in advance how to communicate with your stakeholders. If you took the time to identify and prioritize your stakeholders as we suggested, you have a good starting point. Next you and your team should agree on a communication plan, the largest component of which will generally be a communication matrix. It will include the various stakeholders, what you need to learn from them, what you need to share with them, with what frequency (this can be at regular intervals or when milestones are reached), their preferred communication method, and the person on your team responsible for making sure this happens (often called the *owner* of communication with that stakeholder). This last part is crucial and really does need to be *one* person—even if the information gathered or shared pertains to multiple people—in order to prevent a situation in which everyone claims, "I thought someone else was doing it." You will see this policy of an individual owner again when we discuss risks in Chapter 4.

One thing to keep in mind when deciding which methods of communication to use with various stakeholders is that simple is often

# Exhibit 3.5

## Project Communication Matrix

| Stake-holder | Learn from | Share with | Timing/ Frequency | Method | Owner |
|---|---|---|---|---|---|
| Investor | Return on investment expectations | Project status and main issues | Kickoff meeting, then monthly | Conference calls and email follow-up | Project manager |
| Developer | Construction plans and cost/benefit trade-offs | End-user needs and desires, costs | At start and every 2 weeks | Conference calls and email follow-up | Project manager |
| Construction company | Work progress status and main issues | Construction plans | Every 2 weeks | On-site meetings | Construction site manager |
| Local government | Building rules and standards | Permits requests and construction plans | At start and then as needed | Department official forms | Developer |
| Customers | Needs and Desires | Information | At start, when plans are ready, and when building is ready | Initial market analysis, website, on-site inspections | Marketing agency |

preferable. There are so many modes of communicating, from videoconferencing to e-mails to telephone calls, and they can each be useful under the right circumstances. However, all else being equal, we recommend you go with the simplest and most direct option. In fact, there is much to be said about face-to-face communication when possible, since most communication experts agree that 60 percent to 90 percent of communication is nonverbal depending on the individual and situation.[10] The more direct your communication, the less chance there is that your message will be misconstrued. An example communication matrix is shown in Exhibit 3.5, and a template for a communication matrix is shown in Exhibit 3.6.

## Exhibit 3.6

## Project Communication Matrix Template

| Stake-holder | Learn from | Share with | Timing/ Frequency | Method | Owner |
|---|---|---|---|---|---|
| | | | | | |
| | | | | | |
| | | | | | |
| | | | | | |
| | | | | | |
| | | | | | |
| | | | | | |
| | | | | | |

## Summary

There are a variety of potential sources of conflict inherent to project management. To help mitigate this conflict, as a project manager, you should foster an atmosphere of open communication—with an emphasis on active listening—and lead by example. A project team is made up of full-time workers and part-time SMEs. You will need a plan for acquiring, developing, and managing these workers that includes getting new members brought up to speed quickly and releasing workers once their contribution has ended. You will also need a communication management plan that details how to communicate with your team and with the various project stakeholders. In addition to identifying your project's stakeholders early on, your team should take time to understand and prioritize the stakeholders. That way you will ensure that your key stakeholders' needs are being met.

## Key Questions

1. What issues are typical for project teams in your organization and how do you work through them?

2. How do you acquire, develop, and lead project teams?

3. How do you identify, prioritize, communicate with, and build relationships with project stakeholders?

## Notes

1. Anantatmula (2016), p. 9.
2. Martin (2017), p. 5 and Mindtools (2018).
3. Adapted from Kloppenborg and Laning (2015), p. 352.
4. Ahsan et al. (2013), p. 47.
5. Miller (2008), p. 41.
6. Adapted from Worsley (2017), pp. 9–10 and 92–94.
7. Phillips (2015).
8. Badiru (2008), p. 29.
9. Adapted from Paquette and Frankl (2016), pp. 32–35.
10. The Nonverbal Group (2015).

## References

Ahsan, K., M. Ho, and S. Khan. 2013. "Recruiting Project Managers: A Comparative Analysis of Competencies and Recruitment Signals from Job Advertisements." *Project Management Journal* 44, no. 5, pp. 36–54.

Anantatmula, V. 2016. *Project Teams: A Structured Development Approach.* New York: Business Expert Press.

Badiru, A.B. 2008. *Triple C Model of Project Management: Communication, Cooperation, and Coordination.* Boca Raton, FL: CRC Press.

Kloppenborg, T.J., and L.J. Laning. 2015. *Strategic Leadership of Portfolio and Project Management.* New York: Business Expert Press.

Martin, S. 2017. *Co-Create: Harnessing the Human Element in Project Management.* New York: Business Expert Press.

Miller, S.R. 2008. Building and Managing an Effective Project Team. *Defense AT&L* 37, no. 5, pp. 37–41.

Mindtools. 2018. http://www.mindtools.com/pages/article/newLDR_86 .htm, (accessed May 5, 2015).

The Nonverbal Group. 2015. http://www.nonverbalgroup.com/2011/08/ how-much-of-communication-is-really-nonverbal, (accessed June 13, 2018).

Paquette, P., and M. Frankl. 2016. *Agile Project Management for Business Transformation Success*. New York: Business Expert Press.

Philips, J. 2015. Real World Project Management: Communications. http://www.projectsmart.co.uk/real-world-project-management-communications.php, (accessed February 27, 2015).

Worsley, L. 2017. *Stakeholder-led Project Management: Changing the Way We Manage Projects*. New York: Business Expert Press.

# CHAPTER 4

# Determining What Your Project Will Deliver

Projects are conducted to create something useful. Most of the time, someone wants either a new product or service to be developed or an existing one to be improved. It is essential to understand: what is needed from the project, what all will be included, and how to make sure it is delivered. In this chapter, we discuss how to collect requirements, define scope, construct work breakdown structures (WBSs), plan for risk, and plan for change.

The purpose of this chapter is to help you:

1. Collect specific and useful requirements so you understand what you need to develop on the project.
2. Create a WBS so you know exactly what will be included and what will not be included.
3. Identify risks, assess them to determine which are the major ones, and prepare response plans for the major risks.
4. Establish change control procedures so you consider possible changes, understand their impact, and enforce decisions on whether or not to make the changes.

## Collect Requirements

A good project manager will keep her paramount objective—satisfying the project's customers—in mind throughout the life of her project. Yet that imperative is not always as simple as it sounds. How do we really know what the customers want? A common source of frustration on projects comes from the fact that often *the customer isn't entirely sure what he or she wants.* Even when the customer does have a good idea of what he wants, he does not always do an adequate job of conveying his desires to the project manager and team. Without a clear, universal understanding of what the project hopes to accomplish, your team will be in trouble. Your role as the project manager here: is to understand the problem to be solved and/or opportunity to be capitalized upon; to set up a method for verifying with your stakeholders that they also understand and agree; and to translate that into quantifiable and provable requirements. These requirements should be stated in terms of capabilities that users will have from the deliverables you create on your project.

As the project manager, you need to lead your team through the process of collecting requirements from the project's stakeholders. Since you have already worked as a team to create a project charter, you have a couple advantages at this point: everyone should have at least a cursory understanding of what the project is and why it is being undertaken, and you've already taken time to identify and rank your stakeholders, so you know whose needs must be met for your project to be successful.

To *collect requirements* means you will learn from your customer and any other key stakeholders exactly what they need from your project. These requirements could be *project* requirements that they expect from the project itself, or *product* requirements which will apply specifically to your deliverables. While collecting requirements is, like so many other project management tools and processes, scalable (and will be more detailed and laborious the larger your project is), it is a critical step that should never be skipped even on the smallest projects. The requirements you gather will form the basis for your WBS, which we will discuss later in this chapter. The WBS, in turn, will serve as the foundation for creating your schedule and budget.

Some of the most common requirements gathering tools and techniques are as follow:

- Questionnaires
- Brainstorming sessions
- Meetings and/or interviews with stakeholders
- Focus groups
- Prototyping

Again, depending on the size and scope of your project, you may use one or several of these techniques. You will need to compile the requirements into a database or list that is easily referred to. While asking direct questions of your customers and other stakeholders is a great way to gather requirements, keep in mind that their initial answers may not be specific enough and may require for you to ask follow-up questions. The best requirements will be specific, quantifiable, and easy to measure. In other words, at any step along the project life cycle, you should be able to quickly ascertain whether or not you are meeting the project requirements. For example, requirements for an inventory project may include the following, each of which would have a specific goal and method of measuring defined:

- Well-defined end-user requirements
- Increased inventory accuracy
- Increased inventory turnover
- Reduced inventory holding costs
- Better customer response/flexibility
- Smooth delivery of product to customer

One last point bears mentioning here. While it is your job as a project manager to understand and try to meet your key stakeholders' expectations, you also need to make sure everyone on your project is being realistic. If a customer or other stakeholder has a completely unrealistic or improbable hope for the project, you need to find a way to delicately bring him or her back to reality. Remember, you will be held accountable for meeting clearly defined and agreed-to expectations. Why would you set yourself up for failure by agreeing to expectations you know are not feasible? While it is decidedly uncomfortable delivering negative news to an important stakeholder, it is greatly preferable to do it now rather than to disappoint someone at the end of a project by not delivering what they were expecting.

On larger, more complex projects, in addition to documenting your project requirements, you may also need to come up with a requirements management plan and a requirements traceability matrix which follows each requirement from project inception to successful completion of the project. A requirements management plan describes how requirements will be gathered and shared so stakeholders can preview them and offer feedback.[1] A requirements traceability matrix shows the business need, requirements, and stakeholders. It could also show the priority of each requirement and perhaps how and when it will be measured. Exhibit 4.1 is a requirements traceability matrix.

## Exhibit 4.1

## Requirements Traceability Matrix

| Business Need | Requirements | Stakeholder(s) | Priority |
|---|---|---|---|
| Monetary savings | Standardized equipment | Finance Department | High |
| | Replacement plan | Operating Department | |
| Safety | Equipment risk rate | Maintenance Department | Very high |
| | Safety reporting system | Risk Management Department | |

For Agile projects, the product owner represents customers, so their wishes can be understood and to the extent possible, satisfied. The product owner captures the customer's requirements as stories using the format:

- As a (or as the) _____
- I want _____
- So that _____.

For example, the project of developing a new performing arts center described in Chapter 2 might include:

- As a drama teacher at McKinley High School
- I want a 600 seat theater with conveniences
- So that we can stage great productions that will wow the community.

# Define Scope

Once everyone shares a clear understanding of your project's requirements, it is time to return to your scope definition. The more time and effort you originally spent on this part of the project charter, the farther along you will be now. Basically what you need to do now is refer back to the original charter and make sure it aligns with your detailed requirements. If it does not, you need to update your original scope statement. Keep in mind, the scope refers to what is included—and what is *not* included—in your project. Think of the scope as establishing the boundaries of what your project hopes to accomplish, and feel free to include in your scope statement a list of things that are not part of your project scope if that helps your stakeholders arrive at a common understanding. Remember that as part of your scope you must also include acceptance criteria that are easily measured.

Sometimes a stakeholder wants you to include features that you believe should not be included. If your project is one in a series, sometimes you can satisfy that stakeholder by honestly saying that a particular feature they want will not be in this project but will be considered for the next project.

## Scope and Project Life Cycle

If your project scope is fixed, the traditional, Waterfall project life cycle might be what you would choose to use. If scope is negotiable, an Agile project life cycle may make more sense. If you do use Agile, all of the requirements will still be collected up front, and the total is called the product backlog. The product owner will determine for each sprint what part of the requirements backlog is most important and will negotiate with the scrum master and project team how much of the backlog will be produced during the upcoming sprint. They do this by "grooming" the backlog—that is, breaking it down into small enough stories that each can be estimated and the team can determine how much they will commit to performing in the upcoming iteration. This is essentially developing the same information traditional projects do, as is described later in the WBS.

## Constraints and Assumptions

Some other things you need to revisit at this point are project constraints and assumptions. A *constraint* is "a limiting factor that affects the execution of a project,"[2] while an *assumption* is "a factor in the planning process that is considered to be true, but is without proof.[3]" We mentioned these in Chapter 2 and hopefully they found their way into your charter. If so, you should briefly review these as a project team and see if any need updating. If they were not included in your original charter, now is the time to add them to your project scope statement. It may seem that constraints and assumptions are so "obvious" there is no point including them, but that is exactly the kind of thinking that leads to problems.

Keep in mind that if your team members come across a situation they are unfamiliar with, in the absence of a clear mandate they will either do *nothing* or do what they *think* needs to be done. Either of these choices can prove problematic. Agreeing ahead of time on some of your constraints and assumptions (A 40-hour work week? Construction delayed when raining?) can prevent this from occurring. That said, no one can foresee every detail of a project, and a good project manager will foster a culture of open communication and demonstrate a willingness to ask and answer questions throughout the project life cycle. If your team members know you will not belittle or harangue them for asking for clarification when needed, they will feel more comfortable speaking up and will not resort to making their own—sometimes costly—assumptions. A few assumptions and constraints are shown as follows:

*Assumptions:*
- Marketing initiatives will be successful.
- Public acceptance will be sufficient.
- Enough people will volunteer.
- An office will be donated for Saturday sessions.
- Attendees will understand lessons.

*Constraints:*
- There may not be enough capital raised.
- The sessions must happen between 15 April and 1 May.
- Sessions cannot last more than 2 hours.

# Work Breakdown Structure

## Creating the Work Breakdown Structure

The WBS is one of the most well-known project management outputs. Its name can be misleading because it does not deal with *work activities* but rather with project *deliverables*. The WBS is a way of dividing and subdividing projects down into manageable chunks called work packages. There are different ways to represent WBSs, though if you use software such as Microsoft Project, you will ultimately end up with an indented list.

To create the WBS, you should refer to your project scope statement and list of requirements. You should hold a brainstorming session with your entire project team and anyone else who will be performing the project work (this is an excellent time to involve subject matter experts [SMEs] because they will know better than anyone else the various components that make up each deliverable). The process used to create a WBS is called decomposition. As the name implies, it involves breaking down the overall project into organized pieces, then further subdividing those pieces down to a level that is small enough to manage (one rule of thumb is that the lowest level work packages should be able to be completed by one person in one day). While items in the WBS are nouns (things), they often need one or more adjectives to differentiate them from each other so that no two items are listed in identical language. For example, you might have *first draft report, second draft report,* and *final report* or *left balcony, center balcony,* and *right balcony.*

The brainstorming session can be captured in a variety of formats, such as indented outline and free format. Remember, you are not focusing on activities yet, just deliverables, so use nouns rather than verbs! The indented outline is shown in Exhibit 4.2. A second is the free form as shown in Exhibit 4.3. While the indented outline is used as input for a software program such as Microsoft Project, many teams find the other, the more visual free form method easier to use when there is a great deal of uncertainty about the project initially. Note on both, the first section is for planning and managing the project. If one forgets all of this work, the project will be behind schedule and over budget before it even begins! Both of these types of format are demonstrated (for the same project).

## Exhibit 4.2

## Indented Outline Format of WBS

**New Product Development Project**
1.0  Project Management
    1.1  Meetings
    1.2  Reports
    1.3  Misc.
2.0  Data Gathering
    2.1  Personal Preferences
    2.2  Consumer Trends
    2.3  General Research
    2.4  Friend Interviews
3.0  Survey Development
    3.1  Data Summary
    3.2  Company Needs
    3.3  Survey Construction
4.0  Pilot Testing
    4.1  Test Group
    4.2  Initial Findings
    4.3  Final Survey

For some projects with a high level of uncertainty, some deliverables or subprojects may not yet be understood enough to be planned. In this case, we will use the Agile technique of rolling wave planning, using decomposition where we can, and saving more detailed planning for the time at which more is understood. This is not a way of getting around adequate planning since it will still be planned in advance of the work being performed; rather, it is a way of admitting we do not have all the information at this time and recognizing our limitations by leaving room in our future schedule to revisit the detailed planning.

### Ensuring Participation

Since creating the WBS is so important, and the more people who help brainstorm the more complete the decomposition process will be, it is

## Exhibit 4.3

## Free Form Format WBS

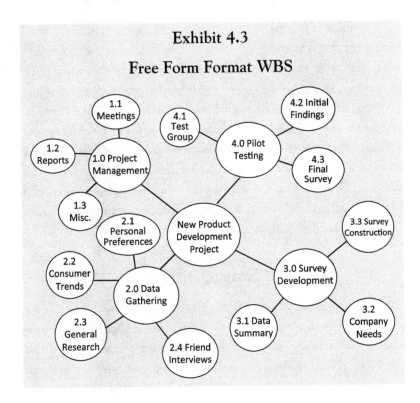

imperative that your team turn out to participate in creating the WBS. Some of your team members may view the work breakdown as unnecessary—especially, if the project involves work they are quite familiar with—and it is your job as project manager to convince them otherwise. Here are a few ways to do that:

- Remind your workers that the WBS will be used to create the project schedule and that *they will* be held to the schedule they set (so it is in their best interest to be as thorough as possible).
- Get people out of their typical environment if possible by meeting off-site so they are not tempted to sneak away to their desks.
- Bring food!
- If possible, create a template of the WBS to begin with (perhaps providing the first group of subheadings, for example) to give the team a starting point.

If a worker is still averse to participating in the creation of the WBS because she claims to know exactly what needs to be done, feel free to borrow the following reply: "Yes, I realize you know exactly what to do, but if you are _____ (hit by a bus/struck by lightning/ out sick), does anyone *else* know what needs to be done?" In all seriousness, we create a WBS at least as much to give everyone a uniform view of the work that needs to be accomplished as we do in order to spell out the deliverables needed from any particular workers or department. The WBS also goes a long way toward showing how the various components of a project are interrelated, which will aid us greatly in creating and sticking to a project schedule (Chapter 5).

## Managing Risks

Prior to creating a baseline schedule, you also need to spend some time brainstorming and planning for risks. In project management terminology, risks are *positive* or *negative* events that may happen and, if so, would affect your project. Risks are inherent to every project, and it is not your goal to avoid risks altogether. Positive risks represent opportunities you want to capitalize on, while negative risks are threats you would like to prevent or minimize.

The planning we are about to suggest focuses on preventing or mitigating negative risks. Like many other project management planning processes, planning for risk should begin with a brainstorming session. Your project team, as well as any SMEs you include, should begin by identifying any and all potential risks to your project. It may help to consult your project charter and other planning documents you have so far. When we lead this brainstorming session with students or clients, we have participants use a Post-it note for each risk identified, no matter how small or far-fetched. (Remember, one rule of a brainstorming session is to include all answers.)

Project risks will fall into one of three categories: known knowns, known unknowns, and unknown unknowns (also called unk unks). Known knowns are comprised of the risks that can be most easily foreseen. This may sound like an oxymoron, since we stated above that uncertainty is inherent to risks. Yet that degree of uncertainty can vary widely. For instance, a common known known in the construction industry is rain. Although we cannot predict with much accuracy *when* it will rain over the course of a project that lasts several weeks or months, it is almost certain—at least in most climates—that it will rain at some point. Something less likely but still well within the realm of possibility is a known unknown. Sticking to our construction example, a known unknown may be a blizzard, if you live in a climate where that is possible but infrequent.

Finally, unknown unknowns are the types of risk that, frankly, you don't even see coming. They involve a previously unforeseen threat such as a supplier going out of business, geopolitical changes that affect your project, death of a key stakeholder, and so on. You may be wondering: *How can I plan for something I cannot even predict?* In short, there isn't much you can do—especially at this stage of risk identification. However, the very existence of unknown unknowns will be taken into account in Chapter 6 when we get to budgeting for the project. For now, we want you to know about all three categories of risks, but we realize you will only be able to identify and plan for the known knowns and known unknowns.

Once your team has identified as many project risks as they can come up with and listed them, one per Post-it note, you will discuss as a team how to rank each risk according to two criteria: probability of the risk happening and impact if it does. If your team did a thorough job in the brainstorming session, you should have identified more risks than it makes sense to address. Therefore, we are going to create risk response plans for only the most likely and/or devastating risks. Create a line graph, with one axis showing probability on a low to high scale, and the other axis depicting impact, again low to high. Draw a diagonal line from the left upper quadrant to the right lower quadrant. Any risks your group rates above this line will require a risk response plan; the risks below the line will be noted but not dealt with at this time. The diagonal line you draw does not need to be right down the middle; you can shift it right/up if your sponsor has a high degree of risk-tolerance or left/down if he or she is risk-averse. You should discuss this tolerance level with your sponsor, and you may need to remind an extremely risk-averse sponsor that it is not our goal to avoid risk entirely (since it would be cost-prohibitive and inefficient to do so).

Next, as a group you take each Post-it note risk you identified and agree where on the scale it should be placed. It is important to do this as a group, since different people will have different opinions and viewpoints about how to categorize the various risks. Exhibit 4.4 is an example showing major risks above the sponsor's acceptance line and minor risks below the line.

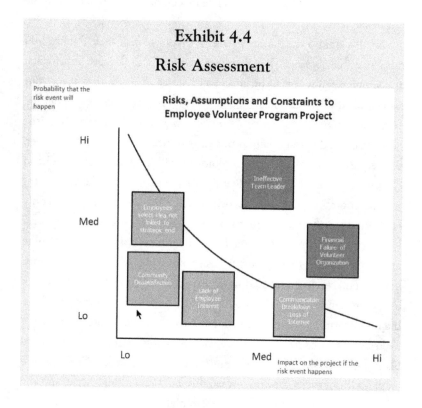

### Exhibit 4.4

### Risk Assessment

Once each Post-it has been added to the graph, you will need to come up with a risk response plan, to lessen the impact or probability of each risk that is above the line of risk-tolerance. These risk response plans do not have to be elaborate, but they do each need one and only one owner, that is, the person who will be in charge of implementing the response plan if and when necessary. Exhibit 4.5 shows a response plan for the two major risks shown in Exhibit 4.4. The information in this response plan should be maintained and updated as conditions change. This document is often called a risk register and any additional information you choose to identify and store concerning risks can be added to the risk register.

Agile projects conduct stand-up meetings every morning with the entire team to discuss what each member plans to do that day and any risks they foresee. Agile projects also use retrospective meetings at the end of each iteration, in which they ask what the team can do better on future iterations. Each of these types of meetings helps to reduce risks by increasing awareness and giving everyone a chance to offer ideas.

## Exhibit 4.5

## Risk Response Plan

| Risk | Plan | Owner |
|------|------|-------|
| Ineffective Team Leader | 1. Councilor champion share team lead<br>2. Bi-weekly reports expected<br>3. Clearly enunciated responsibilities | Project Manager |
| Financial Failure of Volunteer Organization | 1. Ensure self-funding<br>2. Select strong, financially stable partners | Sponsor |

## Establishing Change Control

We are nearing the point at which the actual work of our project will begin. This work will be based on our baseline project schedule, and all the planning documents we have created so far will help to generate this schedule. Once our schedule is agreed to, we will be held accountable for delivering results according to its time, scope, and budget. So, whereas the charter we made during the initiating process group was a living document and easily changed if agreed to, the project schedule will serve as a point of reference that is not easily adapted. Any changes we make after agreeing to the project schedule run the risk of *scope creep*, or expanding the parameters of our project without adding time or money. To prevent this, we need to create and stick to a well-defined, documented change control system.

This may sound intimidating, but it can actually be quite simple. The bottom line is that you need a method of documenting changes. Once the project schedule is agreed to, any change needs to begin with a written change request, which will be approved or not by the project manager, sponsor, or customer. (Decide in advance with your sponsor or customer which changes are small enough for you to decide unilaterally and which are large enough that she would like to weigh in.) If changes are made, make sure they are communicated to everyone who needs to know them and that any expected impact to schedule, budget or other facet is clearly documented. As the project manager, *you* are responsible for setting the expectation that even small changes go through the written change request process. An example of a change request form is shown in Exhibit 4.6.

Agile projects handle change differently. Each iteration is planned just before it starts with as much information as possible. Once the team commits to creating certain deliverables during an iteration, very little change is allowed within that iteration. However, the team—with concurrence from the product owner—may elect to make even radical changes from one iteration to the next. Remember, this is still a structured way to propose, understand, and decide to make (or not make) a change.

## Exhibit 4.6

## Change Request Template

Date proposed:
Description of proposed change:


Why is the change needed?


Impact on: Scope:
Impact on: Schedule:
Impact on: Quality:
Impact on: Risks:
Impact on: Team:

Date approved by:

Project Manager                 Sponsor              Customer
_____          _____        _____

Now that our deliverables have been broken down into work packages from our WBS and we've generated plans for addressing risks and changes, it is time to begin scheduling our project. That is what we'll be doing in Chapter 5.

## Summary

In order for your project to be successful, you and your team must first reach a deep, common understanding of what your project will accomplish. You do this by collecting requirements from the various stakeholders—with an emphasis on the needs of the key stakeholders, when necessary. You will put the agreed-upon requirements into a WBS that will help you organize and break down the overall project work into smaller deliverables. The lowest level of the WBS is comprised of work packages.

In addition to understanding the work required by the project, you and the rest of your team also need to understand the risks involved. Not all project risks are foreseeable, but you should brainstorm as many threats to your project as possible and invest some time and effort into mitigating or eliminating the greatest risks to your project. Finally, your project team needs a standardized way of requesting, approving, implementing, and communicating changes throughout the life cycle of the project.

## Key Questions

1. How do you collect specific and useful requirements so you understand what you need to develop on the project?

2. How do you create a WBS so you know exactly what will be included and what will not be included?

3. How do you identify risks, assess them to determine which are major, and prepare response plans for the major risks?

4. How do you establish change control so you consider possible changes, understand their impact, and enforce decisions on whether to make the changes or not?

# Notes

1. James (2015).
2. *PMBOK Guide* (2017), p. 701.
3. *PMBOK Guide* (2017), p. 699.

# References

Hoogveld, M. 2018. *Agile Management: The Fast and Flexible Approach to Continuous Improvements and Innovations in Organizations.* New York: Business Expert Press.

James, V. 2015. *Leveraging Business Analysis for Project Success.* New York: Business Expert Press.

Paquette, P., and M. Frankl. 2016. *Agile Project Management for Business Transformation Success.* New York: Business Expert Press.

*PMBOK Guide.* 2017. *A Guide to the Project Management Body of Knowledge*, 6th ed. Newtown Square, PA: Project Management Institute.

Vanderjack, B. 2015. *The Agile Edge: Managing Projects Effectively Using Agile Scrum.* New York: Business Expert Press.

# CHAPTER 5

# Project Scheduling

Remember how in Chapter 4 we pointed out that the work breakdown structure (WBS) breaks the project down into *deliverables* rather than *activities*? Well now comes the time when we define the actual activities needed to be performed to complete the project. As you may have guessed, we will use the lowest level deliverables from the WBS—the work packages—as inspiration. Creating the project schedule is incredibly important because once your sponsor approves it, the schedule will serve as a baseline for all the project work you and your team perform. You will be judged based on how well your project is able to stay on schedule as well as on the project's cost and quality.

A realistic project schedule considers several possible limitations. First, there may be a logical order in which some activities can be performed and we address this first by sequencing the activities. Second, each activity takes a certain amount of time and we cover this by estimating how long each activity will take. We will show the schedule on an easy-to-read Gantt chart. Third, we may not have all of the specific people we need exactly when we need them. We address this by assigning workers to each activity and then looking at all of the assignments to see if anyone is overloaded. If they are, we try to reduce the problem by comparing the assignments with the schedule. Fourth, some project schedules are limited by cash flow, which we address in the next chapter.

The purpose of this chapter is to help you:

1. Create a project schedule by defining and sequencing work activities into a network schedule and then identifying the critical path.
2. Communicate the project schedule simply by using a Gantt chart.
3. Assign a worker to each activity, identify where worker demand is overloaded, and resolve some of those overloads by "playing Tetris."

## Defining Work Activities

During this stage of planning, it is essential that you involve the people who will actually be performing the project work, whether they are team members, subject matter experts (SMEs), or others. Whoever it is needs to have a high degree of understanding about what the project entails. By looking at each work package, they should have a good idea of what needs to be done to complete each deliverable according to the acceptance criteria. In this way, you will generate a lengthy list of all the various activities that comprise your project.

List each activity on its own Post-it note, and make sure that each activity has a name (the more self-explanatory, the better!) that is short and begins with a verb. The more people you involve in this process, the more thorough your list will be. And although it may be difficult or time-consuming to involve many people—especially from a wide variety of disciplines or departments—it will be time and energy well-spent. Remember, your schedule will be based on these activities, so any forgotten activities risk delaying your project and making you look bad. Exhibit 5.1 is an example of an activity list.

## Exhibit 5.1

## Activity List

- Purchase wood (PW)
- String electrical wires (SEW)
- Install railings (IR)
- Assemble ramp (AR)
- Hang paneling (HP)
- Install fixtures (IF)
- Paint all wood (PAW)
- Turn on electricity (TOE)

## Sequencing Work Activities

Once your activities have been defined, it is time to sequence them. Again, let the more knowledgeable members guide the rest of the team through this process. Since each activity is listed on a Post-it note, use a table or wall to begin putting them in logical order; put any activities that can start immediately (in other words, they don't depend on any other project activities to be completed) at the far left of your table or wall. Put activities that you know will take place toward the end of the project at the far right. Using the collective judgment and experience of the team, determine logical orders for each and every activity you have. Show the relationships between activities with arrows, with the work of the project flowing from left to right chronologically.

Note that each activity can have more than one *predecessor activity* (which must be performed *before* it) and/or more than one *successor activity* (which cannot be performed until after the given activity). Keep in mind that you are not yet factoring in such logic as how many workers you have or how many activities can realistically be performed simultaneously. For now, it is important that you sequence your activities so that each activity takes place *as soon as possible,* based only on the activities that are its logical predecessors. If more than one activity can begin right away (with no predecessor), create a Post-it note that just says start and have arrows from it go to the activities that can start immediately. The same holds true at the end: if there is more than one activity with nothing following, create a Post-it note that says end. When you calculate the schedule you will understand the value of having a single start and end. An example of this type of sequencing logic for a small project is shown in Exhibit 5.2.

On large projects you will use scheduling software such as Microsoft Project. However, even then, project software requires you to be a knowledgeable user and to identify predecessor and successor activities. Software can do a good deal of the tedious part of scheduling for you, but it cannot read your mind! Unless you tell it otherwise, Microsoft Project will assign each activity its default setting of beginning immediately and lasting a day. As you can imagine, a "schedule" that looks like this would be beyond useless. You, the project manager, need to understand the logic behind the sequencing of your activities. That is important both now, as you are creating a schedule, and throughout the life cycle of your project. When trade-offs have to be made or a project sped up, it is your understanding of the logical sequence and dependencies of activities that will help you make the best decisions for your team and project.

On Agile projects, you can also use Post-it notes to determine the sequence of detailed activities within the iteration you are planning. This visual flow of work can be posted for the entire team to see.

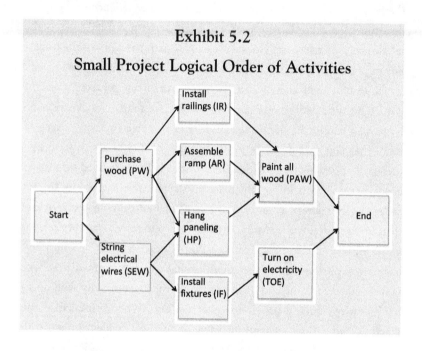

## Exhibit 5.2

## Small Project Logical Order of Activities

## Estimating Activity Duration

Once your activities have been sequenced, it is time to estimate how long each one will take. Yet again, the people who create the estimates should be the ones who will be performing—and therefore understand better than anyone else—the activities at hand. That said, you as the project manager need to have a good enough understanding of the activities or to at least seek a second opinion if you think there's a chance that the estimates are incorrect. Some workers may overestimate the amount of time necessary in order to pad their estimates; these could unnecessarily slow down your project or even prevent you from getting the bid if you are competing for project work. On the other hand, some workers may be overly optimistic about how quickly they can accomplish certain activities; if unchecked, this could set you up for the stress of falling behind schedule and disappointing your customers and sponsor.

Some activities will be much shorter than others, but it is important you use the same unit of time for all. So, decide in advance if you will use weeks, workdays, or hours. Conflicting units of time make scheduling much more difficult and accident-prone. Exhibit 5.3 continues the example started previously with time estimates in work hours shown for each activity in the bottom center of each square. In some fields, such as construction, there are professionally developed standards as to how long certain activities take, scalable to the size of the job. The American Physical Plant Association, International Facility Manager's Association, and others have this information documented in their benchmarking data. If your project is in an industry that has standards such as these, by all means use them!

As an appendage to your activity duration estimates, it is good practice to include any assumptions you made in calculating them, as well as your degree of certainty in the estimates. For example, in creating your estimate for placing electrical wires, did you assume all your diagrams for the building were accurate and up-to-date or did you assume some of the diagrams contain errors, leading you to include additional time to account for the expected difficulties? You may also document *activity attributes,* comprised of such information as predecessor and successor activities, resource requirements, constraints, and so on. All this supplementary information will further help you in our next step: developing the project schedule.

## Developing the Project Schedule

Now that you have created your list of activities, sequenced them, and estimated the time to perform each, you are ready to create your project schedule. We will use the coding system in the lower right corner of Exhibit 5.3 to keep things straight. Each activity name, abbreviation, and estimated duration is put in its own box (also referred to as a *node* in PM terminology).

The outside four corners of each activity box will represent the activity's early start (ES), early finish (EF), late start (LS), and late finish (LF) times (you can use hours, days, weeks, etc. as long as you are consistent throughout). These labels refer to the soonest or latest time an activity can begin and end and are used to determine the project's *critical path*. We will also calculate *float* and place that to the immediate left of each activity box. Float, also called slack, is the amount of flexibility a particular activity has in the schedule. In other words, it is the length of time the activity can be delayed from its ES without delaying the project. As you will see, activities on the critical path will have a float of 0, which means they cannot be delayed without causing a delay to the project. We will show an example in Exhibit 5.4.

If we used software such as Microsoft Project, we would use calendar dates taking holidays and weekends into consideration. When we calculate by hand, we simplify. We say that any activity that can start right away can begin after zero days. This would work just as well if our schedule was in hours or weeks. We will use the two-pass method to calculate our schedule.

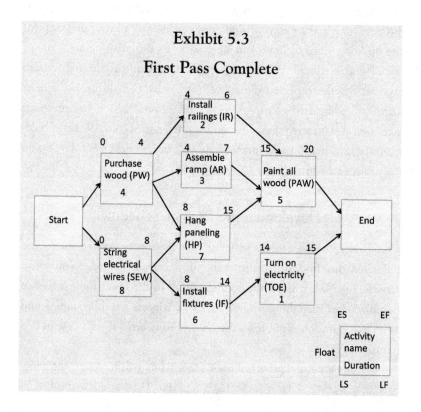

## Exhibit 5.3

## First Pass Complete

### First Pass (Forward)

*Purchase wood* (PW) can start right away (after zero days) and it takes 4 days to complete, so the EF is 4 days. *String electrical wires* (SEW) can also start immediately and takes 8 days, so it has 8 as an EF time. Now an activity that has only one predecessor such as *assemble ramp* (AR), can begin as soon as its predecessor is done. In this case, *AR* can start after 4 days and takes 3 days, so the earliest it can be done is after 7 total days. That is pretty straightforward. However, when an activity has more than one predecessor, you need to allow enough time for each predecessor to be done. For example, *hang paneling* (HP) cannot start until you have purchased the wood *and* strung the electrical wires behind where you plan to hang the paneling. Therefore, *HP* cannot begin until after day 8, when the slower of these two predecessor activities ends. Since it takes 7 days to hang the paneling, this activity can be completed after 15 days. We complete our forward or first pass through the network using this same logic on all our activities. The project end occurs when the last activity is complete—in this case, after 20 days. This is shown in Exhibit 5.3.

### Second Pass (Backward)

The first pass showed us how *soon* each activity could finish. Now we work backward asking how *late* each activity could finish and then how late it could start. Since the project will end after 20 days, the two activities that are last both need to end by then. Therefore, both *paint all wood* (PAW) and *turn on electricity* (TOE) are shown with a LF (in their lower right corners) of 20.

We then subtract the estimated durations from the LF to calculate the LS. For example, *PAW* must end by 20 and takes 5 days, so it must start no later than after day 15. *TOE* takes only 1 hour and since it needs to be completed by day 20, we must start turning it on no later than day 19.

When there is more than one arrow out of an activity, you must allow enough time for each path of activities that follow to be complete. When we did our first pass going forward, if there were multiple predecessor activities, we deferred to the time of the predecessor activity that took longest to complete. Going backward is just the opposite, so we choose the shorter time because it allows all successor activities enough time to finish. For example, all three activities of *install railings* (IR), *AR*, and *HP* depend on purchasing the wood. IR must start no later than day 13. *AR* must start no later than day 12. *HP* must start no later than day 8. Choose the smallest number, day 8, to allow all following activities enough time. If you chose any number larger than day 8, *HP* would be late. See Exhibit 5.4 to see the second pass complete.

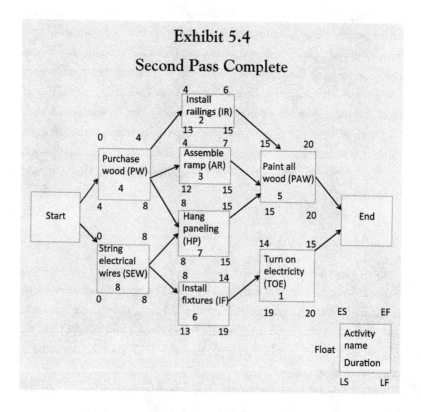

# Exhibit 5.4

## Second Pass Complete

## Identifying the Critical Path

The combination of sequencing and duration estimating give us the critical path—that is the longest series of activities in the project. If we want to complete the project faster, we need to speed up something on the critical path. Conversely, if anything on the critical path is delayed, the entire project is delayed. We now can use our schedule to determine which activities must be conducted exactly when scheduled (those on the critical path) and which ones have flexibility. Again, this flexibility is called float or slack and is shown to the immediate left of the activity. Float is calculated by:

$$\text{Late Start (LS)} - \text{Early Start (ES)} = \text{Float}$$

For example, *AR* could start as soon as 4 days or could be delayed to start as late as 12 days with no impact on the rest of the schedule. Therefore, assemble ramp's float is calculated as $12 - 4 = 8$.

## Exhibit 5.5

## Critical Path Identified

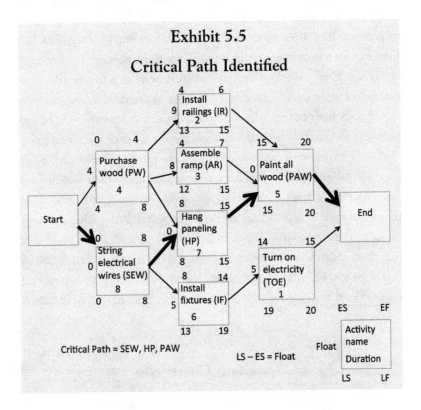

The sequence of activities from start to finish with zero slack is called the critical path and is usually marked vividly (i.e., Microsoft Project denotes the critical path in red). The float for each activity and the critical path are shown on Exhibit 5.5.

## Showing Your Schedule on a Gantt Chart

We need the logic of the network diagram as shown above to *create* a project schedule, but it is not always the best way to *communicate* the schedule. For that we use a simple bar chart called a Gantt chart. To create a Gantt chart, each activity will have its own row, so for our example project, we show *purchase wood* (PW), *SEW*, and so on. We need to create a horizontal scale large enough to read but small enough to show the entire project and consistent throughout, so people looking at it will get the correct impression.

We usually mark critical path activities in red or in bold, if our work is black and white, so people notice them. We draw a bar from ES to EF and mark the times to make it easy for people to read. We do this first for all critical path activities. Then we use blue or nonbold for noncritical activities. We *front-load* the schedule, meaning we use ES and finish times as the endpoints of our bars. Finally, we show the float for the noncritical activities. (Remember, critical activities have no float.) One easy way to do this is to extend a dotted black line out to the LF for the activity, as that represents the end of its float. The Gantt chart for this example project is shown in Exhibit 5.6.

Gantt charts work well whether you are using Waterfall, Agile, or a hybrid project life cycle. However, remember that when working on Agile projects, a team creates their schedule one sprint at a time. One simple example of a roadmap in the Agile world is the schedule for a musician's concert tour as shown in Exhibit 5.7. The idea is to make sure that there are timelines for easy tracking, ownership, and accountability at one glance. Here is a roadmap that shows three sprints with high and detailed level tasks identified that need to be completed during sprints.

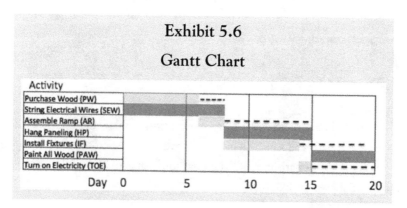

**Exhibit 5.6**

**Gantt Chart**

# Exhibit 5.7

## Agile Example of Gantt Chart

| ID No: | GOALS | HIGH LEVEL | DETAILED LEVEL | 20-Feb | 27-Feb | 6-Mar | 13-Mar | 20-Mar | 27-Mar | 3-Apr |
|---|---|---|---|---|---|---|---|---|---|---|
| Sprint 1 | | | | | | | | | | |
| | Sprint Planning | | | | | | | | | |
| FR1 | | Develop a transportation plan | Land, water and air transpotation for people | ■ | | | | | | |
| FR2 | | | Land, water and air transpotation for equipment | | ■ | | | | | |
| FR3 | | | | | | | | | | |
| | Sprint Review | | | | | | | | | |
| Sprint 2 | | | | | | | | | | |
| | Sprint Planning | | | | | | | | | |
| FR1 | | Formulate a media coverage plan | Acquire and sign contracts | | | | ■ | | | |
| FR2 | | | Activate social media links | | | | | ■ | | |
| FR3 | | | | | | | | | | |
| | Sprint Review | | | | | | | | | |
| Sprint 3 | | | | | | | | | | |
| | Sprint Planning | | | | | | | | | |
| FR1 | | Stage Management | Build Lighting team | | | | | | ■ | |
| FR2 | | | Build Sound team | | | | | | ■ | |
| FR3 | | | Build Costumes team | | | | | | | |
| | Sprint Review | | Build Props team | | | | | | | |
| Product Sponsor: | xxxxxx | | | | | | | | | |
| Product Owner: | xxxxxx | | | | | | | | | |
| Team leader | xxxxx | | | | | | | | | |

Source: Raji Sivaraman

# Assigning Workers

Once you have identified all the work activities needed to create your project deliverables, you will want to assign responsibility for completing each. Further, you will want to ensure that all necessary communication and approvals take place. An easy way to do this is with a matrix called a RACI chart. RACI is an acronym standing for responsible, accountable, consult, and inform.

A good practice is to have only one person accountable for the results of a given work activity. That may or may not be the person who is responsible for performing the work. Frequently the project manager is accountable for many of the activities even though other team members may be responsible for performing some of the tasks. Similarly, on a few major items, the sponsor may have accountability while the project manager has responsibility. A myriad of other stakeholders may need to be consulted for their opinions or at least informed of what transpires.

When constructing a RACI chart, the first column is the name of the activities. The remaining columns are for the various stakeholders. In our example, we will keep it simple with just the sponsor, project manager, and two core team members. Frequently, there will be quite a few more stakeholders. Sometimes a stakeholder has no involvement and no need to be informed of a particular activity like Bill on *SEW* as shown in Exhibit 5.8.

## Exhibit 5.8
## RACI Chart

| Work Package or Activity | Sponsor | Project Manager | Brenda | Bill |
|---|---|---|---|---|
| Purchase Wood (PW) | A | R | | |
| String Electrical Wires (SEW) | I | C | A | |
| Install Railings (IR) | | A | R | I |
| Assemble Ramp (AR) | | C | C | A |
| Hang Paneling (HP) | | A | C | R |
| Install Fixtures (IF) | I | A | R | R |
| Paint All Wood (PAW) | | I | I | A |
| Turn on Electricity (TOE) | I | A | R | C |

## Identifying Resource Overloads

Remember that there are multiple constraints that can limit how fast a project can be completed. The emerging schedule you have created with a network diagram and then shown on a Gantt chart is based upon two of those limiting factors: the estimated duration of each individual activity and the logical order in which you can perform them. We now turn our attention to a third constraint: the availability of the right workers when you need them.

We will continue to use the same example. For simplicity sake, let's say we have two workers and either can do any of the activities. We now want to discover if we have scheduled more than two workers at the same time and, if so, what can we do about it. We will use the same scale as the

Gantt chart and construct a histogram showing the demand for workers directly beneath the Gantt. When we glance at the Gantt, it appears that sometimes we might have scheduled three workers, so we will make our histogram three workers high.

We begin by placing the critical path activities on the bottom row. The reason for this is we might have to change when some activities are scheduled, *and we know we do not want to change the critical path as that would delay the entire project.* The first activity on the critical path is SEW. Therefore, the first block of work shown is one worker high by 8 hours long and SEW is shown in that block. That is followed by the other two critical path activities, *HP* from 9 to 15 and *PAW* from 16 to 20. Now we begin to stack simultaneous activities vertically. *PW* also takes one worker and its ES and EF go from time zero to four. *AR* follows at four to seven. *IR* would need a third worker from four to six, so it is built up to the third row. *Install fixtures* (IF) from 9 to 14 and *TOE* on day 15 would also be on the second row above *HP*. We have an overload shown with need for a third worker from hours 4 to 6. This is all shown in Exhibit 5.9.

## Exhibit 5.9
## Worker Overloads Identified

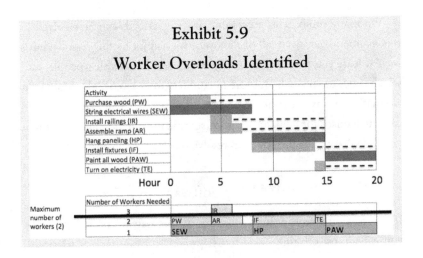

Remember that we scheduled everything as early as possible. Therefore, we cannot move anything earlier, but we can move activities later if they have enough float and still complete the project on time. To do this, we essentially "play Tetris." In that game, you try to fit shapes into spaces.

We will try to delay activities while remembering their logical order and amount of float. In our example, if we delay the start of *IR* 3 days, it can be rescheduled for the second worker after *AR* is complete. That would mean we need to delay *IF* and *TOE* a day each, as there was only space for a day after *AR* (day 8) in the original schedule. Each of these activities had more float than the 1 or 2 days we used up by delaying them. This is all shown in Exhibit 5.10.

## Exhibit 5.10
## Worker Overload Resolved by Playing Tetris

| Number of Workers Needed | | | | | |
|---|---|---|---|---|---|
| 3 | | | | | |
| 2 | PW | AR | IR | IF | TE |
| 1 | SEW | | | HP | PAW |

On many projects, at least some of the overloads can be resolved in this manner. Even when all of the overloads cannot be fully resolved this way, at least you now know exactly which activities, which people, and which times of your schedule are in conflict. You can consider looking at alternative means to further resolve conflicts. Finally, you may need to go to your sponsor for help, armed with specific information and proof that you did what you could to try to resolve the conflicts in advance.

## Using Software

If you have not been doing so already, at this stage in project planning you will almost certainly want to use project software such as Microsoft Project. As long as you have accurate data to provide, the software will help you aggregate information from many of your planning documents, including:

- Activity List;
- Activity Duration Estimates;

- Activity Attributes;
- Project Schedule Network Diagrams—the logical relationships of predecessors and successors you came up with during *Sequence Activities*;
- Activity Resource Requirements—the types and quantities of resources needed for each activity;
- Resource Calendars—include typical days and hours worked and individual workers' schedules (vacation time, maternity leave, etc.);
- Project Scope Statement—we include this because it details the constraints and assumptions that may affect our project;
- Risk Register (you created this in Chapter 4);
- Project Staff Assignments—specify which resources are assigned to each activity.

## Summary

You will use the work packages from your WBS to determine the actual activities that need to be accomplished to complete your project and how long each activity will take. Logic will help you decide the order in which to accomplish the various activities, and the sequence of activities that lasts the longest from start to finish will be your critical path. Throughout the execution of your project you must take care not to delay activities on the critical path unless absolutely necessary since any change to the critical path will delay your overall project.

Only after you have decided on the order of activities will you begin assigning them to your human resources. If your schedule shows more activities taking place simultaneously than your workforce can accommodate, you have a resource overload and must find a way to adapt the schedule—if at all possible, without making changes to the critical path as not to delay the project. Use the two-pass method detailed in this chapter to determine the critical path and float/slack of all noncritical activities.

## Key Questions

1. How will you create a project schedule by defining and sequencing work activities into a network schedule and then identifying the critical path?

2. How will you communicate the project schedule simply by using a Gantt chart?

3. How will you assign a worker to each activity, identify where worker demand is overloaded, and resolve some of those overloads by "playing Tetris"?

# CHAPTER 6

# Budgeting and Baselining Your Project

Projects are investments. In the charter, we started to look at the benefits of a project, and in the work breakdown structure (WBS), we looked in more depth at exactly what we will create with the project. Now it is time to understand what it will cost us to create all of those deliverables. During project selection and chartering, very rough estimates of cost were considered to determine if the project's benefits are likely to be worth the investment. Now, in the detailed planning, more comprehensive cost estimates are developed to once again determine if the project's benefits are worth the investment. Additionally, the project budget will be used to manage cash flow and guide decisions about how to use resources on the project.

Project planning is iterative and, as such, you would likely do a bit of budgeting before you determine all the details of scheduling, assigning workers, and planning for risks. For convenience, we will cover all of the cost estimating and budgeting work in this chapter, but keep in mind that you generally need to finalize the other planning before you can finalize the budget. We will also describe at the end of this chapter how to consolidate the schedule, budget, scope, risk, and resource plans into one integrated whole.

The purpose of this chapter is to help you:

1. Estimate all project costs at the level of detail needed.
2. Assemble all of the costs into a time-phased budget that can be used for project control.
3. Consolidate the completed schedule, budget, scope, risk, and resources into an integrated project plan, which you will use to baseline and then kickoff the project.

# Estimate Cost

The completeness and accuracy of the inputs you have in terms of scope, WBS, schedule, and resources will largely determine how accurate your project budget will be.

## Costs and Sustainability

In estimating project costs, we estimate not only how much it will cost to create all of the project deliverables, but how much it will cost to use them for their intended life span and then to dispose of them responsibly. This is called life cycle cost and has become important as more people and organizations have begun to focus on sustainability.

In the spirit of sustainability, we now frequently use the triple bottom line when we consider project investments, that is, *how will this project impact people, planet, and profit?* Projects have always sought to generate profit. This has been considered directly in the form of costs (usually in trade-offs with schedule and performance). In recent years, project managers have become more attuned to the needs and desires of various stakeholders including suppliers, customers, neighbors, regulating authorities, team members, and so on. The triple bottom line dictates that we understand the costs (financial and other) to each of these stakeholders. *Planet* is the third part of the bottom line. While some things we may do to help the planet are expensive, other ways of trying to protect the planet can save us money. For example, careful planning helps us to use our resources more efficiently, and considering the life cycle cost of what we create may allow for operational and disposal cost savings that more than offset production cost increases. In addition, this life cycle cost approach is consistent with the *Project Management Institute's Code of Ethics and Professional Conduct* in respect to the values of responsibility, fairness, and honesty.[1]

## Types of Costs

Costs can be divided simply into direct costs and indirect costs. Direct costs will not be incurred unless the project is undertaken. These include labor and materials. There are often other direct costs such as facilities or equipment that is acquired specifically for a project. Indirect costs, on the other hand, are ones that will be shared by a project, but that the parent organization will incur with or without the project. Utilities and equipment or facilities that are already part of the organization are often treated as indirect costs. These costs are allocated partially to the project and partially to other uses. If project budgets need to be established and monitored in your organization, you should understand what these costs are and how they are determined. Costs can also be divided into fixed costs and variable costs. An example of a fixed cost is purchase of a computer for your project, wherein the cost is the same no matter how much you use it. An example of variable cost is labor, which you pay for each hour of effort.

### Cost Estimating Methods

Three commonly used methods of estimating costs are analogous, parametric, and bottom-up. Analogous estimating means estimating based on data from past, similar work activities. The more similar your past and present projects are—in terms of scope, duration, size, complexity, and so on—the more useful this type of estimate will be. This type of estimating isn't costly and doesn't take much time. You simply compare your upcoming project to a recently completed one and ask how the new project is similar to and different than the previous one. You take the actual cost of the previous project as a starting point and ask how is the new one bigger or smaller, more or less complicated, and how much those differences will impact the cost. The flip side to the benefit of being easy is that analogous estimating is not as accurate as other estimating techniques. Unless your project is simple and/or extremely similar to a past project whose actual cost data is easily referenced, you should probably not rely on analogous estimating as your only tool during this stage. Analogous estimating is often used during project selection, since using ballpark estimates is the only practical method until more project details are decided.

A second common estimating technique used in project management is parametric estimating. Parametric estimating uses historical data and project scope to create a mathematical estimate for duration or cost. For example, on a construction project that is 10,000 square feet, a parametric estimate would multiply the square footage by the given price per square foot to come up with a cost estimate. Or, on a complex software project, you may determine that the average programmer can write 10 lines of code per day, so it will take 80 days' worth of work to complete 800 lines of code. You may go further if you know you have four available workers by deducing that it will take the four of them 20 days (80/4 = 20). Parametric estimating can be quite helpful, but its results are dependent on good data and knowledgeable application.

Parametric estimating can be taken to another level of detail by asking about features in a project that significantly impact cost. For example, if you were determining the cost to build a house, you would take into account not only total square footage, but also the number of bathrooms, whether the kitchen counters will be granite or a less expensive alternative, whether or not the windows will be high efficiency, and so on. These factors collectively will quickly help an estimator develop a more accurate estimate. Depending on the need for accuracy, this may be sufficient or an even more detailed estimate may be needed.

The third method is bottom-up estimating, which includes identifying every element of cost (generally by using the WBS as a reference) and adding them up. This is potentially the most accurate form of estimating as you hopefully include the cost of every single project element. However, it is critical to double check because if any element is missing, that portion of the project is underestimated by 100 percent. Generally some elements of a project are overestimated and others are underestimated and, if the estimator does not have a consistent bias, they may somewhat offset each other. However, if any element is not included, it would take quite a few overestimates to offset it! Many experienced estimators will conduct both a parametric estimate and a bottom-up estimate, so the parametric one can serve as an indicator that something may have been missing from the bottom-up estimate if there is a large discrepancy.

## Contingencies and Uncertainty

If you know that you will need to spend money on a particular item, obviously you should estimate it and include it in your project budget. There are situations, however, in which you may or may not need to spend money. Some are for risks that you can anticipate but do not know if they will happen. You will need to address these as well. Money for these "known unknowns" is called contingency reserve. The contingency reserve is included in your project budget but is held in reserve until and unless needed. An extremely heavy rain in a climate that may or may not experience such a deluge during the time the project is being conducted is a known unknown.

There are other risks on many projects that are just not envisioned. These "unknown unknowns" are things that seem to come out of the blue. Money for these is considered management reserve. It is not estimated directly—and therefore not included in the project's budget, but must be considered part of the funding requirements. Therefore, project managers need to forecast based on the history of similar projects about how much extra money should be included for management reserve. Generally, before this money can be spent, a project manager needs to justify it with a change order and a sponsor may need to approve it. An earthquake that is completely unexpected where the project is being conducted is an example of an unknown unknown.

### Value Engineering

If by the time you have estimated all of your costs and considered both types of contingencies, your organization does not have enough money to fully fund your project, one alternative is to conduct value engineering. That is, review the entire project by asking if all of the features and functions are truly necessary and also asking if there is a less expensive way to accomplish any of the project goals. Value engineering may slow the project planning, but it will often save significant money by eliminating nice-to-have features and using alternative approaches.

## Determine Budget

Many projects are constrained by money—both overall and/or on a cash flow basis. Therefore, it is important to understand how the budget will impact both the overall project scope and the day-to-day schedule.

### Aggregating the Budget

To establish a project budget, you first must know what all of the project deliverables are (identified in the WBS), what activities are required to create those deliverables (identified and put into chronological order in

Chapter 5), and when each activity is scheduled. Some activities have only variable cost such as labor, while other activities have both fixed cost (such as equipment) and variable cost. We will continue with the same example we used to demonstrate scheduling. Some activities will have fixed costs and all will have variable costs. For simplicity, the fixed costs will be assigned when the activity starts, while variable costs will be assigned for each day of work. The overall project budget is $17,400 as can be seen in Exhibit 6.1.

### Cash Flow

Exhibit 6.2 shows the cash flow needed for the project. This example shows the original schedule (*without* certain activities delayed to level the resource demands). The first part of the exhibit is a Gantt chart that shows when each activity is scheduled. Note the vertical lines denoting weeks. Many project budgets are divided into either weeks or months. Directly below the Gantt chart is a table showing the cost for each activity on a weekly basis. For example, the first activity (PW) has $3,000 of fixed cost and $400 of variable cost ($100 per day for four work days) assigned in the first week for a total of $3,400. The next activity, string electrical wires (SEW) spans two time periods with the fixed cost and 5 days of work in the first week and the remaining 3 days of work in the second week.

### Budgets as a Basis for Control

The costs for all of the activities are shown both on a weekly and a cumulative basis. Since there are four activities in the first week, the total cost is $8,500. In the second week, an additional $4,200 is budgeted, so the cumulative total for the first 2 weeks is $12,700. This cumulative budget will form the basis of cost control. Note that this project requires quite a bit of cash early on, as there are significant fixed costs for some of the materials during the first week. If the required amount of cash is not available that soon, some activities (and likely the entire project) will need to be delayed. A total cost curve is depicted in Exhibit 6.3 to show the cumulative budget. In Chapter 7, we will use this cumulative budget with earned value to show how to determine how well your project is doing in terms of both cost and schedule.

## Exhibit 6.1

## Project Total Cost Example

| Activity | Fixed Cost (FC) | Variable Cost (VC) Per Day | Number of Days | VC | Total Cost (TC) |
|---|---|---|---|---|---|
| PW | 3,000 | 100 | 4 | 400 | 3,400 |
| SEW | 1,000 | 600 | 8 | 4,800 | 5,800 |
| IR | 500 | 300 | 2 | 600 | 1,100 |
| AR | 0 | 300 | 3 | 900 | 900 |
| HP | 0 | 300 | 7 | 2,100 | 2,100 |
| IF | 100 | 400 | 6 | 2,400 | 2,500 |
| PAW | 300 | 250 | 5 | 1,250 | 1,550 |
| TOE | 0 | 50 | 1 | 50 | 50 |
| | | | | | 17,400 |

## Exhibit 6.2

## Project Cash Flow Example

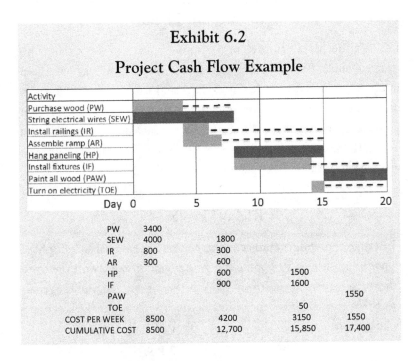

| Activity | | | | |
|---|---|---|---|---|
| Purchase wood (PW) | | | | |
| String electrical wires (SEW) | | | | |
| Install railings (IR) | | | | |
| Assemble ramp (AR) | | | | |
| Hang paneling (HP) | | | | |
| Install fixtures (IF) | | | | |
| Paint all wood (PAW) | | | | |
| Turn on electricity (TOE) | | | | |

Day    0          5          10          15          20

| | | | | |
|---|---|---|---|---|
| PW | 3400 | | | |
| SEW | 4000 | 1800 | | |
| IR | 800 | 300 | | |
| AR | 300 | 600 | | |
| HP | | 600 | 1500 | |
| IF | | 900 | 1600 | |
| PAW | | | | 1550 |
| TOE | | | 50 | |
| COST PER WEEK | 8500 | 4200 | 3150 | 1550 |
| CUMULATIVE COST | 8500 | 12,700 | 15,850 | 17,400 |

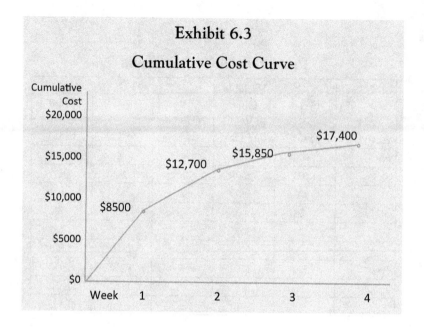

## Exhibit 6.3
## Cumulative Cost Curve

# Consolidate Schedule, Budget, Scope, and Resources into Integrated Plan

It is now time to put all parts of your project plan together into one integrated whole. If your project is small and simple, you may have been integrating cost, schedule, resources, risks, and scope all along. However, on more complicated projects, sometimes different people plan different portions. If so, put them all together and ensure they make sense as a whole. If you are conducting your project using the Agile method, you will consolidate all of these plans at the start of each iteration.

# Kickoff Project

On a large or prominent project, there may be a ceremonial kickoff/photo opportunity such as a ribbon cutting or groundbreaking with the company president and a golden shovel. Whether or not your project generates this type of publicity, the most crucial parts of a project kickoff occur behind the scenes.

When you are ready to transition from project planning to execution, you should gather your project team, sponsor, and as many key stakeholders as possible for a kickoff meeting. There you will review the project plan, assign responsibilities, and generate excitement about starting the actual project work. Try to make the project kickoff as festive as you can.

## Baseline Consolidated Project Plan

Once all of your stakeholders have agreed to your project plan, you should consider the plan a commitment. You have promised to create the listed deliverables to the agreed-upon quality standards, by the agreed-upon date, for the agreed-upon budget, and with the agreed-upon resources. Now you need to deliver on your promises! Again, if you are doing an Agile project, you are committing for each iteration what you will deliver.

The concept of baselining is helpful here. All of the planning documents were drafts until the entire lot was approved. A baselined plan means that from this point forward if anyone requests a change, the request will need to go through a change management process (discussed in Chapter 7) and, if approved, the impact on budget and schedule will change the baselined plan. Just as the baselined plan means the project manager and team need to deliver as promised, the stakeholders cannot change their minds now without paying for their decision. Thus, the baseline protects both the people conducting the project and the stakeholders of the project.

## Summary

The three types of cost estimating used in project management are analogous, parametric, and bottom-up. You should use one or more than one of these, depending on your project's size and level of detail needed, to create a cost estimate of all the project work you will be performing. Be sure to consider indirect costs as well as direct costs and to include both contingency and management reserves proportionate to the risk involved in your project.

In addition to creating an overall budget for your project, you will need to factor in the issue of cash flow. In other words, *when* do your costs need to be paid and *how* can you pay them on time to prevent a project delay? Once your project budget is complete, you should consolidate it with your other project plan components, namely, the schedule, scope, resource, and risk subplans. Together, these will make up your baselined project management plan that you will use to conduct the rest of the project work and which can only be changed through a formal change control system.

## Key Questions

1. What methods do you use to estimate all project costs at the level of detail needed?

2. How do you assemble all of the costs into a time-phased budget that can be used for project control?

3. How do you consolidate the completed schedule, budget, scope, risk, and resources into an integrated project plan which you baseline prior to project kickoff?

## Notes

1. PMI Code of Ethics (2018).

## References

Goodpasture, J. 2010. *Project Management the Agile Way: Making it Work in the Enterprise.* Fort Lauderdale, FL: J. Ross Publishing.

Maltzman, R., and D. Shirley, D. 2011. *Green Project Management.* Boca Raton, FL: CRC Press.

PMI Code of Ethics. 2018. https://www.pmi.org/about/ethics/code, (accessed June 20, 2018).

Venkataraman, R., and J. Pinto. 2008. *Cost and Value Management in Projects.* Hoboken, NJ: John Wiley and Sons.

# CHAPTER 7

# Directing Project Performance

In order to complete project work, a project manager needs to continue to plan, both because there may not have been enough detail for all the required planning in the first place and because things change. The project manager needs to direct the work of the project team; monitor and control that work; and ensure that the quality is shaping up. As project manager, you maintain momentum on the project by monitoring and controlling risks, controlling the schedule and budget, and controlling changes. Project managers need to spend a substantial amount of their time managing communication, both by understanding communication needs and by utilizing appropriate methods. Finally, project managers need to close the project by transitioning deliverables to customers; capturing and using lessons learned; and managing a handful of post-project activities.

The purpose of this chapter is to help you:

1. Direct and control the project work and the quality of the deliverables.
2. Maintain project momentum by controlling risks, schedule, budget, and changes.
3. Maintain effective project communications and successfully close the project.

## Continued Planning and Directing

Remember some projects are planned in detail before they start (Waterfall) and others have only high-level planning for the entire project at the start with more detailed planning in increments (Agile). Many projects can be considered hybrids, using a bit of both methods, with the results of early work providing the needed information to plan later work in detail. That means many projects will require planning for later work as early work is being completed. Also, most projects will have changes in their environment that necessitate changes in plans. On effective projects, project managers will have at least some planning performed in advance but will also have flexibility to conduct additional planning as it is helpful.

### Directing Project Work While Managing the Team

On many projects, the project manager may personally perform some of the work activities and usually instructs project team members to perform other activities. Included in this work are to:

- execute work activities;
- create project deliverables;
- provide, train, and manage the project team;
- obtain, manage, and use needed resources;
- perform approved changes; and
- do all of this while using approved standards.[1]

Hopefully the project plans have identified the needed people and other resources for the project. However, the project manager needs to continue to make sure each is available when needed and often needs to mentor some of the project team members. One of the standards a project manager should adhere to is whatever ethical guidance is provided within her organization. Some of the actions sponsors take to help project managers during project implementation, a project manager can in turn do on a more limited basis to help project team members. These include empowering individuals to make sensible decisions without second-guessing them, managing organizational politics, and removing obstacles to performance.[2]

Project managers can directly help create an atmosphere of trust by clearly communicating expectations and helping team members develop competencies. They can help create trust indirectly by encouraging team members to work together, support each other, find solutions together, make decisions collectively, and resolve conflicts among themselves.[3]

## Monitoring and Controlling Project Work

Monitoring a project means continually gathering information and using it to determine how well the project is progressing. Controlling project work is comparing actual work with what was planned and, if the difference is great enough, making needed adjustments. A project manager can accomplish both of these partially by spending little bits of time frequently (often daily) with people doing the project work. Seeing first-hand exactly what is happening is so helpful when making decisions. Some of this work can be accomplished using various tools such as earned value analysis (EVA). We will discuss EVA later in this chapter.

The sooner a project manager realizes a potential problem is brewing, the easier it generally is to solve. Therefore, wise project managers create:

1. a culture on their projects in which people are encouraged to quickly admit a potential delay or quality problem may be starting;
2. a method of clearly and quickly communicating the issue; and
3. a method of providing rapid help.

One method of accomplishing this is the use of a visible cue such as red cards. A worker who feels an activity he is performing may cause problems with either deliverable quality or another activity in the schedule posts a red card near his workstation and the project manager promises that either she or someone else will be there within 30 minutes to collaborate on solving the problem.[4]

## Ensuring Quality

There are two approaches to quality and both are needed. Quality assurance is proactively doing the right things such as having good systems and well-trained workers in place; using adequate materials and machines; and fostering an improvement mind-set in which project team members are always asking what is working that can be repeated and what is not working that be changed. Quality assurance is a forward-looking, managerial approach. Done well, it not only helps to create good quality, but also convinces (assures) stakeholders that the project work is well-planned and the present project manager and team are competent.

The other approach is quality control. This is more technical and backward-looking. Quality control involves looking at a specification and asking if the deliverable in question conforms to that specification. This is the test of whether the project products have been completed correctly. If a project team does a good job with quality assurance, quality control should mostly confirm that the work has been done correctly.

## Maintaining Momentum

To maintain momentum on a project, a project manager and team need to control risk, schedule, budget, and changes.

### Monitoring and Controlling Risks

During both initiating and planning, the project team identified possible risks, assessed them to determine which were great enough to have response plans in place in advance, and created response plans for those big risks. Throughout the entire project, a wise project manager and team periodically do those same three activities to:

1. identify more risks that may become known now but were not known during original planning;
2. assess all identified risks to determine if they are significant enough to justify response plans; and
3. create response plans when appropriate. Note, some earlier identified risks may now move from small to big with changing conditions and now need response plans.

Additionally, throughout the project, team members should be assigned to monitor each of the big risks. If there are multiple big risks, it is good practice to have each team member assigned to monitor one or two of the risks rather than make one person keep track of all of them. The person in charge of a particular risk can benefit from looking at an early warning sign, or trigger, that the risk event is about to happen. For example, on a construction project, an early warning sign of severe weather can be a weather forecast. In the same way, for each big risk the person responsible should ask: *What is an early warning sign and how can I continue to monitor it?*

Once a risk event is imminent, the response plan should be put in place. It is often cheaper and easier to respond quickly than after a major problem happens. However, many times a risk event happens without early warning and a team needs to immediately put a response plan into place. Even worse, a risk event may happen that has no predetermined response plan and the team needs to quickly develop and implement a response.

## Exhibit 7.1

## Earned Value Analysis Terms and Definitions[5]

| Term | Acronym | Definition | Determination/ Calculation |
|---|---|---|---|
| Planned value | PV | the amount of work expected to be done if on schedule | From aggregated budget |
| Earned value | EV | the amount of work that is done | From progress reports |
| Actual cost | AC | how much the completed work costs | From progress reports |
| Budget at completion | BAC | how much the entire project should cost | From aggregated budget |
| Schedule variance | SV | how much the project is ahead (+) or behind (−) schedule | $SV = EV - PV$ |
| Cost variance | CV | how much the project is under (+) or over (−) budget | $CV = EV - AC$ |
| Schedule performance index | SPI | how efficient the project is so far in terms of schedule | $SPI = EV/PV$ |
| Cost performance index | CPI | how efficient the project is so far in terms of budget | $CPI = EV/AC$ |
| Estimate to complete | ETC | how much more we expect to spend to finish the project | $ETC = (BAC - EV)/CPI$ |
| Estimate at completion | EAC | how much we expect to spend all together by the end of the project | $EAC = AC + ETC$ |
| To complete performance index | TCPI | how efficient we need to be to complete the project on budget | $TCPI = (BAC - EV)/(BAC - AC)$ |

# Exhibit 7.2

## Earned Value Example Illustrated

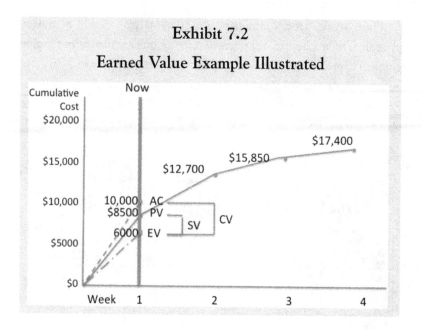

### Controlling Schedule and Budget

EVA is a technique used to monitor both schedule and budget at the same time. It is important to understand that a project can be doing well on one dimension and OK or poorly on the other. For example, a project could be ahead of schedule but either right on budget or over budget. Depending on your sponsor's wishes, doing well on one and poorly on the other may be OK, but usually doing poorly on both is not. Some project sponsors are so eager to have a project completed, that if you can finish it early, they are willing to pay more than the original budget. Understanding your sponsor's desires helps a project manager make decisions based upon EVA.

There are many terms used in earned value that require understanding. Exhibit 7.1 lists, briefly defines, and describes how to determine or calculate each of the terms. We will continue to use the same example project to understand schedules and budgets. The cumulative budget is depicted by the line graph in Exhibit 7.2 and the various earned value terms are shown. We will now demonstrate how each is determined.

From the project budget developed in Chapter 6 and shown on the graph, we can see that by now we should have spent and received value (PV) of $8,500 and we can also see that our budget for the entire project (BAC) is $17,400. We can see that we have actually spent (AC) $10,000 and the value of the work that was completed as of now (EV) is $6,000. Neither is exactly as planned (PV). Now let's calculate how good or bad we are doing by using the formulas in Exhibit 7.1 and use those calculations to help us predict how we will do overall on the project if we continue our current trends.

$$SV = EV - PV$$

$6,000 – $8,500 = -$2,500 (Behind schedule as we have accomplished less than planned)

$$CV = EV - PV$$

$6,000 – $10,000 = -$4,000 (Over budget as we have spent more than planned)

$$SPI = EV/PV$$

$6,000/8,500 = 70% (We have accomplished only 70 percent of what we planned to date)

$$CPI = EV/AC$$

$6,000/10,000 = 60% (We have received only 60 cents worth of value for every dollar spent to date)

$$ETC = (BAC - EV)/CPI$$

($17,400 – 6,000)/.6 = $19,000 (If we continue at our present efficiency, it will cost us an additional $19,000 to complete the project—more than our entire original budget!)

$$EAC = AC + ETC$$

$10,000 + 19,000 = $29,000 (If we continue at our present efficiency, the total project will cost $29,000—way more than our budget of $17,400!)

$$TCPI = (BAC - EV)/(BAC - AC)$$

($17,400 – 6,000)/(17,400 – 10,000) = 1.54 (We would need to improve our efficiency from our current 60 percent immediately to 154 percent to complete the project on budget—a tall order indeed!)

Perhaps when you first looked at Exhibit 7.2 you thought the project was just a little behind schedule and just a little over budget, but no big deal. EVA helps you understand early in a project how your present rate of completing work and spending money can be used to predict what your achievement will be by the time the project ends. It is a very powerful tool. If there are problems, the sooner in a project they are discovered, the sooner adjustments can be made to get back on track.

### Controlling Changes

Many things change during the life of a project, and it is critical to understand which potential changes make sense and which do not. Agile projects handle changes mostly by planning just one iteration at a time in great detail and trying hard not to accept any changes within the iteration. Thus, changes are incorporated into planning for the next iteration, and sometimes on Agile projects the team makes substantial changes from one iteration to the next.

Waterfall projects, on the other hand, often create plans for the entire project at the outset and need to respond to changes occasionally. Good practice on these projects is that all potential changes need to be requested along with the projected impact they may have on the project. Weighing these criteria, a decision needs to be made whether or not to accept each change. If the change request is accepted, the impacts to budget, schedule, and anything else need to be incorporated into updated plans and communicated to all impacted stakeholders. If the change is not accepted, the project manager needs to communicate that decision as well and make sure the person who wanted the change does not try to sneak it in anyway.

Since many people are busy when working on projects, it is much easier for a project manager to ask people to use simple change request forms such as the one shown in Exhibit 7.3. Note this form asks what the requested change is, why it is being requested, what impact it may have, and who will approve it.

## Exhibit 7.3

## Project Change Request

Date Proposed: October 15, 2015

Description of proposed change: Purchase wood from different supplier

Why is the change needed? The original supplier is both very late and way over the original budget.

Impact on Scope: none

Impact on Schedule: 3 day delay

Impact on Budget: save $2000.

Impact on Quality: none

Impact on Risks: may lessen, as first supplier is unreliable

Impact on Team: none

Date approved by:

Project Manager          Sponsor          Customer

_____     _____     _____

We will continue to use the same project example. Remember, from our EVA we discovered we were both behind schedule and over budget. The carpenter is requesting permission to purchase wood from a different supplier. If this is considered a minor request, the project manager should be allowed to make the decision, but if it is major, it might go to the sponsor. If the project is being conducted for an external customer, perhaps that customer might want to retain the right to make the decision. It would be wise to agree in advance what decisions the project manager will be able to make and what decisions will be reserved for the sponsor or customer.

## Manage Communications

In your project planning, hopefully you developed a communication matrix as shown in Chapter 3. This outlines who you need to learn from and share with, along with logistical questions such as the most effective timing and methods and who on your project team is responsible. Now that you are implementing the project, it is time to more fully understand the communication needs and to utilize the appropriate methods to fulfill those needs.

### Understanding Communication Needs

Many decisions need to be made on projects, and these require accurate, transparent, and timely information. The project manager, team members, sponsor, and other stakeholders all need to make decisions. A key judgment is knowing when enough information is in hand to make the necessary decision. Projects often have significant time pressure, and decisions may need to be made before all information is available.

Remembering that the most important success factor in projects is customer success, wise project managers try to keep their customers involved throughout the project. This requires frequent communication and effort. If the project manager and team show an eagerness to communicate and collaborate, stakeholders will believe they have first-hand, undistorted information, and they will trust the project manager and team.

## Communication Barriers, Topics, and Benefits

Although people know communication on projects is essential, communication is frequently more limited than ideal because of barriers such as the following:

1. **Lack of understanding:** people often work in silos, do not understand others' needs, have had limited orientation, or do not realize the impact of certain communications.
2. **Priorities:** too much work, difficulties with the pace required, issues inherent with multi-tasking, and the basic fact that some people do not like to read.
3. **Complexity and size:** complicated, potentially confusing projects that have large, varied, and/or dispersed teams.
4. **Methods:** people may not know how to communicate in certain situations or understand the technology that is used.
5. **Meeting management:** meetings can be disorganized; long; poorly facilitated; and/or may have limited outcomes.
6. **Culture:** can refer to culture of the parent organization as well as differences in culture among project team and various stakeholders. These conflicts can lead to limited trust, respect, and/or care for others.
7. **Fear:** of conflict, asking questions, upsetting others (especially senior officials), or creating or being given more work.

Some topics are especially useful yet are not discussed openly enough or in a timely fashion. Some of these subjects include:

1. **High-level goals:** purpose of project, impact of project, who will benefit from project, business need, critical success factors, and the impact of not achieving project goals.
2. **Tactical goals:** schedule, milestones, deliverables, quality, and cost.
3. **Expectations:** reasons "why," expectations of participants, work needed to complete a task, and follow-up with accountability.
4. **Status/progress:** progress, cost, up-coming milestones, resource concerns, constraints, mistakes, what is working and why, approved changes.

5. **Personnel:** people not pulling their weight and other human resource issues.
6. **Risk:** issues, constraints, roadblocks, challenges, uncertainty, and contingencies to address them.

If people do a good job communicating on their projects, many groups will benefit, including:

1. **Individuals working on the project:** increased motivation, encouragement, ownership, and loyalty.
2. **Project members as a team:** having healthy conflict, respect for others, sense of community, and better meetings.
3. **Stakeholders:** continued engagement, better relationships, and improved future prospects.
   Some general benefits that often result include:
4. **Decision making:** more efficient, producing better solutions, innovation, less confusion, fewer surprises, and greater accuracy.
5. **Performance:** better value, less rework, risks resolved, improved change management, and better problem visibility.
6. **Speed:** of actions, making decisions, and meeting schedules.

## Using Appropriate Communications

Three types of communications are especially effective for project managers: face-to-face conversations, stand-up meetings, and progress reports. Effective project managers spend a bit of time nearly every day in informal conversation with both their team and with various stakeholders. Many little things are discussed that would likely not be brought up in a formal report or meeting. Also, these frequent, informal chats are great for relationship building.

Although stand-up meetings have been used in many situations, they have been popularized with Agile projects. The idea is to have the project team get together daily for a short (perhaps 15 minute) meeting. As the name suggests, these meetings are intended to be short enough that no one should take a seat or get too comfortable! Each team member tells what he did the previous day, what he plans to do this day, how his work relates to other work, and any risks or issues he foresees. The meeting is not used to solve problems, but often two people who need to work together will do so right after the meeting.

Both face-to-face conversations and stand-up meetings can be more difficult when a project team is virtual. However, effective project managers will still attempt to accomplish the same goals of frequent exchange of information and relationship building using whatever means and timing they can.

Most project sponsors and customers want to be assured on a regular basis that the project is progressing well. For this reason, progress reports are often used. Progress reports may be used with or without earned value as described earlier. They may also be effective if used with an updated Gantt chart to show how much progress has been made on each activity. An updated Gantt chart for our example project in Exhibit 7.4 shows that the second activity, String electrical wires (SEW), is one day ahead of schedule (shown by the bar color turned to black). Since that activity is on the critical path (denoted by the bold bar), that is good. However, the first activity, Purchase wood (PW), has not even started and is now 5 days behind schedule. That also means that the next two activities, Install railings (IR) and Assemble ramp (AR), are also not started as they need the wood.

One simple way to consider project progress is to look back at the previous time period, directly at the current time period, and forward to the remainder of the project. We will continue to use our example project to demonstrate this in Exhibit 7.5. This progress report spells out much of the detail behind the updates shown in Exhibit 7.4.

The time periods for this project are in weeks. Let us look back at the end of the first week. In this example, we were ahead on one activity (SEW) and behind on three others (PW, IR and AR) that were scheduled for this week. We start by reminding our sponsor or customer what they had approved for us to do during this time period and then compare that to what we actually accomplished. Any difference is a variance. Variances can be good or bad—ahead or behind schedule, over or under budget. In this example, we were 5 days behind on noncritical activity *PW*, but one day ahead on critical activity SEW. Although we are pleased to be ahead on the critical activity, we are 5 days behind on an activity with only

4 days of slack, so the project is a day behind. Because we do not yet have the wood, the next two activities are delayed.

We then look at the current time period, considering our actual progress to date, not just what we originally planned. For each activity (or milestone if you are reporting at the milestone level), we want to tell our sponsor about any risks that we are concerned about and any issues that will need to be decided. Since one supplier has held up an activity, we may need to consider a replacement. Also, one route for the ramp requires a bush to be removed, and we want the customer to make that decision. If we need to have a change approved from our original plan, now is the time. In our example, we need to find a new wood supplier and purchase the wood very quickly, and this will require approval.

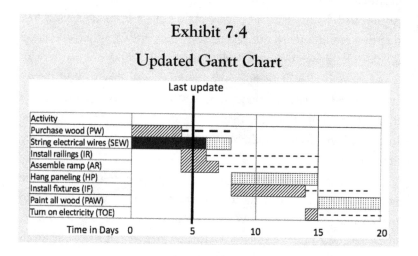

## Exhibit 7.4

## Updated Gantt Chart

Most of our customers are quite concerned with when the project will be done (and often how much it will cost). For this reason, we project the remainder of the project at this point. Two of the remaining activities are not on the critical path, so we are OK with saying they will be behind the original schedule, but will still be completed in plenty of time. The other two activities (*Hang Paneling* [HP] and *Paint All Wood* [PAW]) are on the critical path. If we can save one day on either one, we will finish on schedule. We have noted the risk that speeding these activities up may entail.

When a project is making good progress, these reports are simple. When a project is in trouble, these reports generate the kind of discussion

# Exhibit 7.5

## Progress Report

### Past Time Period

| Activities | Approved Plan | Actual Progress | Variances | Causes |
|---|---|---|---|---|
| Wood purchased | 4 days | Not started | 5 days behind | Failed supplier |
| Electric wires strung | 5 of 8 days | 6 days complete | 1 day ahead | Bob on a roll |
| Railings installed | 1 of 2 days | 0 | 1 day behind | Wood delay |
| Assembled ramp | 1 of 3 days | 0 | 1 day behind | Wood delay |

### Current Time Period

| Activities | Plan Until Next Report | Risks Before Next Report | Issues Before Next Report | Changes to Approve |
|---|---|---|---|---|
| Wood purchased | All 4 days | New supplier | | New supplier |
| Railings installed | 2 days | New wood supplier | | |
| Electric wires strung | Remaining 2 days | | | |
| Assembled ramp | 3 days | New wood supplier | Move bush? | |
| Paneling Hung | 1 of 7 days | New wood supplier | | 1 day delay to CP |
| Fixtures Installed | 3 of 6 days | | | |

### Future Time Period

| Activities | Plan to Completion | Risks After Next Report | Issues After Next Report | |
|---|---|---|---|---|
| Paneling hung | Day 16 | May be hard to save 1 day | | Try to save 1 day, on CP |
| Fixtures installed | Day 13 | | | OK, not on CP |
| Wood painted | Day 20 | May have to save 1 day if paneling not accelerated | | Try to save 1 day, on CP |
| Electricity turned on | Day 14 | | Seek earlier approval? | |

that uncovers problems and helps to either get the project back on track or at least to give people realistic expectations going forward. We want to share any bad news early enough that adjustments can be made and the project can still be successful.

# Close Project

The point in time when project execution gives way to project closing is when the primary customer accepts the primary project deliverable. It is helpful to think of this as a transition rather than a single point in time. Project managers also want to capture and share lessons learned and to complete a few necessary post-project activities.

## Transitioning Deliverables

We want to create satisfied and capable customers. If you have kept your customer involved throughout the project, the deliverables are likely to be useful to them. We want to help the customer ensure that the deliverables work correctly and that the promised benefits are achieved. This may require some assistance in the form of demonstrations, instructions, training, and/or a website with frequently asked questions. A well-satisfied customer can be one of the most effective ways to secure future projects. It may be worthwhile after the deliverables have been used for some time (perhaps a few weeks or months) to assess how fully they have delivered on the promises that were made.

## Capturing and Sharing Lessons Learned

The end of the project is a terrific time to ask what worked well that should be repeated on a future project and what could be done better on future projects. Capturing the lessons can be as simple as asking each team member to identify one thing that went well to be repeated in the future and one thing that should be done differently. Capturing lessons can be more involved also by reviewing project documents to follow the progress from creating the charter on through the project's life cycle and asking at each point, what was learned. Project teams can do this on their own, and they can also ask customers, sponsor, and other key stakeholders for feedback.

These lessons should then be organized by topic and stored somewhere that is convenient for people planning and managing future projects. The lessons can be written very briefly, but a good practice is to include the name and cell phone number of the person who submitted the lesson, so future project managers can have an informal conversation when trying to apply the lesson. If your organization has a project management office (PMO), they should instruct you where and how to archive the lessons learned.

### Completing Post-project Activities

Project managers want to make sure they provide feedback on the work of their project team members to their respective supervisors. This may be informal since the supervisor probably is the person who formally evaluates his or her direct reports, but it is still good practice. There may also be some accounting, materials, equipment, or other issues to finish.

## Summary

Once the work of your project is underway, your role as a project manager is to monitor the project's progress and ensure it is unfolding as planned. To determine progress, you will use a variety of techniques, ranging from informal communication with team members and stakeholders to quantifying your progress using earned value management (EVM). You will need to keep your sponsor and other stakeholders aware of this progress as well as any changes made to your baselined project plan.

To formally close your project, you must obtain acceptance of your project deliverables from your customer. Additionally, you must also close all administrative work and document lessons learned. Finally, best practice suggests you should assist in providing evaluations of your team members and helping them find new work.

## Key Questions

1. How do you direct and control the project work and the quality of the deliverables?

2. How do you maintain project momentum by controlling risks, schedule, budget, and changes?

3. How do you maintain effective project communications and successfully close the project?

## Notes

1. Adapted from *PMBOK Guide* (2017), pp. 90–92 and 345.
2. Kloppenborg and Tesch (2015), pp. 29–30.
3. Anantatmula (2016), p. 102.
4. Sting et al. (2015), pp. 36–37.
5. Adapted from *PMBOK Guide* (2017), pp. 261–267 and Kloppenborg et al. (2019), pp. 477–480.

## References

Anantatmula, V. 2016. *Project Teams: A Structured Development Approach.* New York, Business Expert Press.

Kloppenborg, T.J., and D. Tesch. 2015. "How Executive Sponsors Influence Project Success." *MIT Sloan Management Review* 56(3), 27–30.

Kloppenborg, T.J., V. Anantatmula, and K. Wells. 2019. *Contemporary Project Management*, 4th ed. Mason, OH: Cengage Learning.

Marnewick, C., and W. Erasmus. 2014. "Improving the Competence of Project Managers: Taking an Information Technology Project Audit." In *Proceedings Project Management Institute Research and Education Conference*, Limerick, Ireland.

*PMBOK Guide.* 2017. *A Guide to the Project Management Body of Knowledge (6th ed.)* Newtown Square, PA: Project Management Institute.

Sting, F.J., C.H. Loch, and D. Stempfhuber. 2015. "Accelerating Projects by Encouraging Help." *MIT Sloan Management Review* 56, no. 3, pp. 33–41.

# APPENDIX 1

# Templates

These are the templates to accompany *Project Management Essentials*. Each is described in the referenced chapter or appendix.

## Chapter 1

*Project Success Template*

| Success Measure | Relative Importance | How Measured | When Measured |
|---|---|---|---|
| Customer success | | | |
| Satisfaction | | | |
| Use of deliverables | | | |
| Meeting agreements | | | |
| Performance | | | |
| Time | | | |
| Cost | | | |
| Other | | | |
| Business | | | |
| Participants | | | |

## Project Life Cycle Roles and Responsibilities

| Role | Initiating | Planning | Executing | Closing | Later |
|------|------------|----------|-----------|---------|-------|
| Sponsor | | | | | |
| Project manager | | | | | |
| Project manager's boss | | | | | |
| Core team | | | | | |
| Subject matter expert | | | | | |
| Other | | | | | |

# Chapter 2

*Project Charter*

Project Charter

Project Title _____ Date _____

**What** (Scope Overview) (2 to 4 sentences about what is included and what is not)

**Why** (Business Case) (2 to 4 sentences with ROI, alignment, emotional appeal, ethical imperative)

**When** (Milestone Schedule and Acceptance Criteria)

| Milestone | Completion Date | Stakeholder Judge | Acceptance Criteria |
|---|---|---|---|
| Current situation | | | |
| | | | |
| | | | |
| | | | |
| End-of-project situation | | | |
| Ultimate goal | | | |

*Risks*

| Project Risks | Risk Owner | Contingency Plans |
|---|---|---|
| | | |
| | | |
| | | |
| | | |

## Resources Required

| Money | People | Other |
|---|---|---|
|  |  |  |
|  |  |  |
|  |  |  |
|  |  |  |
|  |  |  |

## Routines (Team Operating Principles)

- _____
- _____
- _____

## Communication Needs (Stakeholders)

| Stakeholders | Interest in Project |
|---|---|
| Primary: |  |
| Others: |  |

## Collection of Knowledge (Lessons Learned)

- _____
- _____
- _____

## Commitment

| Sponsor | Date | Signature |
|---|---|---|
|  |  |  |
| Project manager | Date | Signature |
|  |  |  |
| Core team members | Date | Signature |
|  |  |  |

# Chapter 3

*Project Stakeholder Power Interest Grid*

| | | Interest | |
|---|---|---|---|
| | | **Low** | **High** |
| **Power** | **High** | High Power, Low Interest – Keep Satisfied | High Power, High Interest – Manage Closely |
| | **Low** | Low Interest, Low Power – Apathetic | Low Power, High Interest – Keep Informed |

*Project Communication Matrix*

| Stakeholder | Learn from | Share with | Timing/ Frequency | Method | Owner |
|---|---|---|---|---|---|
| | | | | | |
| | | | | | |
| | | | | | |
| | | | | | |
| | | | | | |
| | | | | | |
| | | | | | |
| | | | | | |
| | | | | | |

# Chapter 4

*Requirements Traceability Matrix*

| Business Need | Requirements | Stakeholder(s) | Priority |
|---|---|---|---|
|  |  |  |  |
|  |  |  |  |
|  |  |  |  |
|  |  |  |  |

## Change Request

Date proposed:
Description of proposed change:


Why is the change needed?


Impact on: Scope:
Impact on: Schedule:
Impact on: Quality:
Impact on: Risks:
Impact on: Team:

Date approved by:

Project Manager            Sponsor            Customer
_____           _____          _____

# Chapter 5

## Gantt Chart

| Activity | | | | | | | | | | | | | | | | | | | | | | | |
|---|---|---|---|---|---|---|---|---|---|---|---|---|---|---|---|---|---|---|---|---|---|---|---|
| | | | | | | | | | | | | | | | | | | | | | | | |
| | | | | | | | | | | | | | | | | | | | | | | | |
| | | | | | | | | | | | | | | | | | | | | | | | |
| | | | | | | | | | | | | | | | | | | | | | | | |
| | | | | | | | | | | | | | | | | | | | | | | | |
| | | | | | | | | | | | | | | | | | | | | | | | |
| | | | | | | | | | | | | | | | | | | | | | | | |
| | | | | | | | | | | | | | | | | | | | | | | | |
| | | | | | | | | | | | | | | | | | | | | | | | |

Time

Fill in time for critical activities in red or bold

Fill in time for noncritical activities in blue or muted from early start to early finish

Show slack for noncritical activities as a dashed line from early finish to late finish

## RACI Chart

| Work Package or Activity/Person | | | | |
|---|---|---|---|---|
| | | | | |
| | | | | |
| | | | | |
| | | | | |
| | | | | |

R = Responsible    A = Accountable    C = Consult    I = Inform

# Chapter 6

## Total Cost Spreadsheet

| Activity | Fixed Cost (FC) | Variable Cost (VC) per day | Number of Days | VC | Total Cost (TC) |
|---|---|---|---|---|---|
|  |  |  |  |  |  |
|  |  |  |  |  |  |
|  |  |  |  |  |  |
|  |  |  |  |  |  |
|  |  |  |  |  |  |
|  |  |  |  |  |  |
| Total Cost |  |  |  |  |  |

## Budget Aggregation

| Work Package or Activity/ Time Period | 1 | 2 | 3 | 4 |
|---|---|---|---|---|
|  |  |  |  |  |
|  |  |  |  |  |
|  |  |  |  |  |
|  |  |  |  |  |
|  |  |  |  |  |
| Cost Per Time Period |  |  |  |  |
| Cumulative Cost |  |  |  |  |
|  |  |  |  |  |

# Chapter 7

## *Earned Value*

| Term | Formula | Space for Calculations |
|---|---|---|
| Schedule Variance | $SV = EV - PV$ | |
| Cost Variance | $CV = EV - AC$ | |
| Schedule Performance Index | $SPI = EV/PV$ | |
| Cost Performance Index | $CPI = EV/AC$ | |
| Estimate to Complete | $ETC = (BAC - EV)/CPI$ | |
| Estimate at Completion | $EAC = AC + ETC$ | |
| To Complete Performance Index | $TCPI = BAC - EV)/(BAC - AC)$ | |

## *Progress Report*

| Past Time Period | | | | |
|---|---|---|---|---|
| Milestones | Approved Plan | Actual Progress | Variances | Causes |
| | | | | |
| | | | | |
| **Current Time Period** | | | | |
| Milestones | Plan Until Next Report | Risks Before Next Report | Issues Before Next Report | Changes to Approve |
| | | | | |
| | | | | |
| **Future Time Period** | | | | |
| Milestones | Plan to Completion | Risks After Next Report | Issues After Next Report | Changes to Approve |
| | | | | |
| | | | | |

# Appendix Two

## *Project Selection Matrix*

| Project/ Selection Criteria | Criteria 1 | Criteria 2 | Criteria 3 | Criteria 4 | Total |
|---|---|---|---|---|---|
| Project A | | | | | |
| Project B | | | | | |
| Project C | | | | | |
| Project D | | | | | |

## *Resource Availability Matrix*

| Project/ Resource | Resource 1 | Resource 2 | Resource 3 | Resource 4 |
|---|---|---|---|---|
| Maximum availability | | | | |
| Project A | | | | |
| Project B | | | | |
| Project C | | | | |
| Project D | | | | |
| Remaining availability | | | | |

# APPENDIX 2

# Selecting, Prioritizing, and Resourcing Projects

Good practice for leadership teams in an organization is to first complete strategic planning and then determine the best portfolio of projects and other work that will enable them to achieve their strategy subject to the limits on people and other resources and the amount of risk they are willing to accept. One straightforward way to ensure they select, prioritize, and resource a good portfolio of projects is to use the matrices described here. The first is a project selection matrix. A blank project selection matrix is shown in Exhibit A2.1.

## Exhibit A2.1

## Project Selection Matrix

| Project/ Criteria and Weight | Criteria 1 | Criteria 2 | Criteria 3 | Criteria 4 | Weighted Total Score |
|---|---|---|---|---|---|
| Project A | | | | | |
| Project B | | | | | |
| Project C | | | | | |
| Project D | | | | | |

To choose projects with a selection matrix, an accord must be reached as to the most important criteria for undertaking a project. For example, is it projected ROI? Feasibility? Competitive advantage? You should choose a few important criteria, then determine these criteria's importance relative to one another by assigning each a number between 1 and 10 (1 being least important, 10 being most important). An easy way to do this is to determine which criteria is most important first and assign that 10 points. You can have ties if needed. Then ask how important each other criteria is in comparison to the most important one. *It is imperative you determine the criteria and the importance of each prior to introducing potential projects, since otherwise it is human nature to skew the criteria in favor of pet projects—intentionally or not.* Once you have a few weighted criteria, you can start ranking potential projects. On a scale of 1 to 5, how well does each project meet each respective criterion? Suppose everyone agreed up front that *Return on Investment* was the most important criteria, so you gave it an importance weight of 10. A second criterion, *Customer Relations*, is almost as important, so you give it an importance weight of 8. *Supplier relations* is of medium importance, so you give it an importance weight of 5. *Ease*, on the other hand, is not as important, so you give it an importance weight of 3. After agreeing on these criteria and their respective weights, shown in Exhibit A2.2, the leadership team can now consider individual projects.

## Exhibit A2.2

## Project Selection Matrix with Importance Weights

| Project/ Criteria and Weight | Return on Investment 10 | Customer Relations 8 | Supplier Relations 5 | Ease of Completion 3 | Weighted Total Score |
|---|---|---|---|---|---|
| Project A | | | | | |
| Project B | | | | | |
| Project C | | | | | |
| Project D | | | | | |

Now each project can be rated on each criterion. Perhaps Project A has only a small potential ROI, so you give it a rating of 2 out of 5. It is not labor-intensive, so you give it the maximum rating, a 5, for *Ease*.

Sometimes there is a "must do" project dictated by a government agency or one that is deemed mandatory for some other reason. In those cases, assign a 5 to each criterion so the "must do" project will automatically be the highest priority.

Your last step will be to multiply each rating by the importance criteria, then total the "points" for each potential project. So, for Project A, you will multiply 10 × 2, which is 20. Add 20 to the 3 × 5 (15) and any other weighted criteria. The higher the score for each potential project, the more it aligns with your organization's priorities. That said, since these numbers were assigned subjectively, not everyone may be in perfect agreement. It may make sense to adopt any runaway "winners" such as Project A in this case and put to the side any clear-cut "losers" such as Project B, but to have further discussion about any potential projects with similar, middle-of-the-road scores such as Projects C and D. The completed project selection matrix for this example is shown in Exhibit A2.3.

## Exhibit A2.3

## Completed Project Selection Matrix

| Project/ Selection Criteria | Return on Investment | Customer Relations | Supplier Relations | Ease of Completion | Total |
|---|---|---|---|---|---|
| | 10 | 8 | 5 | 3 | |
| Project A | 2 | 5 | 3 | 5 | 90 |
| | 20 | 40 | 15 | 15 | |
| Project B | 3 | 2 | 1 | 2 | 57 |
| | 30 | 16 | 5 | 6 | |
| Project C | 5 | 1 | 1 | 2 | 69 |
| | 50 | 8 | 5 | 6 | |
| Project D | 3 | 2 | 3 | 3 | 70 |
| | 30 | 16 | 15 | 9 | |

## Prioritizing Projects

The initial prioritization comes from the project selection matrix just described with the projects receiving the most points having the highest priority. However, many times one project is more urgent than others, two projects are related, or other considerations may impact the relative priority. It is wise for the executives who select the projects to explicitly prioritize them, so everyone knows which project gets the priority when there are conflicts.

## Resourcing Projects

Once the prioritization is complete, it is time to assign key resources to projects starting with the highest priority project. These resources can be anything that is in short supply such as key individuals, money, space, or equipment. Once a particular resource is fully assigned, it is fruitless to start additional projects as the conflicts will delay at least one of them. Many times leaders at this point negotiate to move a particular project up in priority. An example of resources needed for the prioritized projects is shown in Exhibit A2.4. Note the projects are listed in the order they were prioritized in Exhibit A2.3.

# Exhibit A2.4

## Project Resources Needed

| Project | Sponsor | Project Manager | Money |
|---------|---------|-----------------|-------|
| Project A | 80 hours | 240 hours | $5 million |
| Project D | 100 hours | 300 hours | $10 million |
| Project C | 130 hours | 400 hours | $17 million |
| Project B | 50 hours | 200 hours | $2 million |

Once we know how much is required for each type of critical resource on each of our prioritized projects, we also need to know how much availability each key resource has (measured in work hours for many resources and dollars for money). We now create one more matrix with availability of each key resource at the top of each column and the projects listed in the order of priority in each row. We assign resources to projects until one type of resource is fully utilized and then we can start no more projects until some of the early ones are completed. In Exhibit A2.5 we start by assigning a sponsor, project manager, and money to the first project and deduct the time or money that project will require to show how much that particular resource has left. For example, the first sponsor only has 70 hours left available, which would not be enough to also sponsor either of the next two prioritized projects. Then we continue to resource the next prioritized project (in this case D) with the required resources of sponsor, project manager and money. Once any of the resources is not

enough for another project, we cannot start any more projects until one
of the existing ones is complete.

## Exhibit A2.5

## Project Resourcing Matrix

| Project/ Resource | Sponsor A | Sponsor B | PM A | PM B | PM C | PM D | Money |
|---|---|---|---|---|---|---|---|
| Maximum availability | 150 hours | 150 hours | 200 hours | 400 hours | 300 hours | 300 hours | $30 million |
| Project A | 80 hours | | | 240 hours | | | $5 million |
| Project D | | | | | | | |
| Project C | | | | | | | |
| Project B | | | | | | | |
| Remaining availability | 70 hours | | | 160 hours | | | $25 million |

# About the Authors

**Kathryn N. Wells**, M.Ed., PMP, is a project management educator who has taught at multiple universities in the United States and abroad. Kathryn has also consulted and trained in project management. She is coauthor of *Contemporary Project Management*, 4th edition and *Project Management for Archaeology* and has produced educational materials used around the world. Kathryn's specialty within project management is residential and investment-based real estate.

**Timothy J. Kloppenborg**, PhD, PMP, is a Professor Emeritus from Xavier University. Tim has over 100 publications, including 11 books, for instance, *Contemporary Project Management*, 4th edition., *Project Management for Archeology*, *Achieving Success in Nonprofit Organizations*, *Strategic Leadership of Portfolio and Project Management*, *Project Leadership*, and *Managing Project Quality*. He has led thousands of people in consulting, training, and university classes on six continents. He is a retired United States Air Force (USAF) Reserve Officer. Tim still teaches short courses in project management and leadership at Xavier University.

# Index

Note: Page numbers followed by "e" indicates exhibits.

# OTHER TITLES IN OUR PORTFOLIO AND PROJECT MANAGEMENT COLLECTION

Timothy J. Kloppenborg, *Editor*

- *Project Management and Leadership Challenges-Volume I: Applying Project Management Principles for Organizational Transformation* by M. Aslam Mirza
- *Innoliteracy: From Design Thinking to Tangible Change* by Steinar Valade-Amland
- *Project Management and Leadership Challenges, Volume II: Understanding Human Factors And Workplace Environment* by M. Aslam Mirza
- *Project Management and Leadership Challenges, Volume III: Respecting Diversity, Building Team Meaningfulness, and Growing Into Leadership Roles* by M. Aslam Mirza
- *Why Projects Fail: Nine Laws for Success* by Tony Martyr
- *Scrum for Teams: A Guide by Practical Example* by Dion Nicolaas
- *Project Management and Leadership Challenges, Volume IV: Agility in Project Management and Collaboration* by M. Aslam Mirza
- *Producing Value from Your Projects the Solent Way* by Paul Summers
- *Project Management Lessons from the World's Greatest Projects and Project Leaders* by Sherif Hashem
- *Developing Strengths-Based Project Teams* by Martha Buelt and Connie Plowman
- *Project-Based Learning: How to Approach, Report, Present, and Learn from Course-Long Projects* by Harm-Jan Steenhuis and Lawrence Rowland
- *Agile Working and the Digital Workspace: Best Practices for Designing and* Implementing Productivity by John Eary

# Announcing the Business Expert Press Digital Library

*Concise e-books business students need for classroom and research*

This book can also be purchased in an e-book collection by your library as

- a one-time purchase,
- that is owned forever,
- allows for simultaneous readers,
- has no restrictions on printing, and
- can be downloaded as PDFs from within the library community.

Our digital library collections are a great solution to beat the rising cost of textbooks. E-books can be loaded into their course management systems or onto students' e-book readers. The **Business Expert Press** digital libraries are very affordable, with no obligation to buy in future years. For more information, please visit **www.businessexpertpress.com/librarians**. To set up a trial in the United States, please email **sales@businessexpertpress.com**.